Driven By Faith: Motor Racing Inspired Christian Life

Joshua Rhoades

Published by Joshua Paul Rhoades, 2024.

While every precaution has been taken in the preparation of this book, the publisher assumes no responsibility for errors or omissions, or for damages resulting from the use of the information contained herein.

DRIVEN BY FAITH: MOTOR RACING INSPIRED CHRISTIAN LIFE

First edition. July 7, 2024.

Copyright © 2024 Joshua Rhoades.

ISBN: 979-8227912404

Written by Joshua Rhoades.

Table of Contents

Chapter 1 Preparation

Preparation is key in both NASCAR and the Christian life, as both require extensive readiness to achieve their goals. In NASCAR, drivers prepare extensively for races. This preparation involves physical training to ensure they are in peak condition, mental exercises to maintain focus and strategy, and technical knowledge to understand the mechanics of their vehicles. Drivers spend countless hours on the track practicing their driving skills, learning the layout of each course, and perfecting their timing. They also work closely with their teams to fine-tune their cars, ensuring that every component is functioning optimally. This preparation is crucial because races are demanding and require not just speed but also precision, endurance, and quick decision-making. Drivers must be ready for any challenges that come their way, from unexpected weather conditions to mechanical failures.

Similarly, Christians prepare for their spiritual journey through prayer and studying God's Word. Just as a NASCAR driver wouldn't enter a race without training, a Christian should not go through life without spiritual preparation. This preparation involves regular prayer, which is a way to communicate with God, seek guidance, and find strength. Prayer helps Christians stay focused on their faith and connected to God, much like a driver stays connected to their team and strategy during a race. Additionally, studying the Bible is essential for understanding God's teachings and applying them to everyday life. 2 Timothy 2:15 encourages Christians to "Study to shew thyself approved unto God, a workman that needeth not to be ashamed, rightly dividing the word of truth." This verse emphasizes the importance of diligent study and understanding of God's Word, which helps Christians navigate life's challenges with wisdom and integrity.

Just as NASCAR drivers need a team of experts to help them prepare, Christians benefit from being part of a community of believers. Fellowship with other Christians provides support, encouragement, and accountability. It helps individuals grow in their faith and stay committed to their spiritual goals. Attending church services, participating in Bible study groups, and engaging in community service are all ways Christians can prepare themselves spiritually. These activities help deepen their understanding of the Bible, strengthen their faith, and build relationships with other believers who can offer support and guidance.

Preparation in both NASCAR and the Christian life also involves setting goals and developing a plan to achieve them. NASCAR drivers set goals for their performance, such as improving their lap times, qualifying for certain races, and ultimately winning championships. They develop detailed plans that include training schedules, practice sessions, and strategies for each race. Similarly, Christians set spiritual goals, such as growing closer to God, overcoming personal struggles, and living out their faith more fully. They develop plans that include regular prayer, Bible study, and involvement in their church community. These plans help Christians stay focused on their spiritual growth and make steady progress toward their goals.

In both scenarios, perseverance is crucial. NASCAR drivers often face setbacks, such as crashes, mechanical failures, and poor race results. However, they persevere, learning from their mistakes and continuing to strive for improvement. Christians also face challenges, such as personal struggles, doubts, and opposition to their faith. Perseverance helps them stay committed to their spiritual journey, trusting that God will guide them through difficult times. James 1:12 says, "Blessed is the man that endureth temptation: for when he is tried, he shall receive the crown of life, which the Lord hath promised to them that love him." This verse reminds Christians of the importance of perseverance and the reward that awaits those who remain faithful.

Another important aspect of preparation is maintaining a positive attitude. NASCAR drivers need to stay positive, even when things don't go as planned. A positive attitude helps them stay focused, motivated, and ready to tackle challenges. Similarly, Christians are called to maintain a positive attitude, trusting in God's plan and remaining hopeful even in difficult circumstances. Philippians 4:8 encourages believers to focus on positive things: "Finally, brethren, whatsoever things are true, whatsoever things are honest, whatsoever things are just, whatsoever things are pure, whatsoever things are lovely, whatsoever things are of good report; if there be any virtue, and if there be any praise, think on these things." This verse highlights the importance of a positive mindset in the

Christian life.

Preparation also involves being equipped with the right tools and resources. NASCAR drivers rely on high-quality equipment, such as their cars, helmets, and safety gear, to perform well and stay safe. They also use advanced technology, such as data analysis and telemetry, to fine-tune their performance. Similarly, Christians rely on spiritual tools and resources, such as the Bible, prayer, and the Holy Spirit, to grow in their faith and navigate life's challenges. Ephesians 6:11-17 describes the "armor of God," which includes the belt of truth, the breastplate of righteousness, the gospel of peace, the shield of faith, the helmet of salvation, and the sword of the Spirit. These tools help Christians stand firm in their faith and resist the temptations and challenges they face.

In addition to personal preparation, teamwork is essential in both NASCAR and the Christian life. NASCAR drivers work closely with their pit crews, engineers, and team managers to prepare for races. Each team member has a specific role, and their collective efforts contribute to the driver's success.

Similarly, Christians are part of the body of Christ, where each member has a unique role and contributes to the overall mission of the church. 1 Corinthians 12:12-27 describes the church as a body with many parts, each with a different function. This passage emphasizes the importance of teamwork and unity in the Christian community, as each member's contributions are valuable and necessary for the body to function effectively.

Finally, preparation in both NASCAR and the Christian life involves continuous improvement. NASCAR drivers constantly seek ways to improve their performance, whether through physical training, mental exercises, or technical advancements. They review their past races, analyze their performance, and make adjustments to enhance their skills and strategies. Similarly, Christians are called to continually grow in their faith and become more like Christ. This involves regular self-examination, repentance, and seeking God's guidance for personal growth. Philippians 3:13-14 says, "Brethren, I count not myself to have apprehended: but this one thing I do, forgetting those things which are behind, and reaching forth unto those things which are before, I press toward the mark for the prize of the high calling of God in Christ Jesus." This verse encourages Christians to keep striving for spiritual growth and to focus on their ultimate goal of becoming more like Christ.

In conclusion, preparation is a crucial aspect of both NASCAR and the Christian life. NASCAR drivers prepare extensively for races through physical training, mental exercises, technical knowledge, and teamwork. Similarly, Christians prepare for their spiritual journey through prayer, studying God's Word, fellowship, setting goals, perseverance, maintaining a positive attitude, using spiritual tools, teamwork, and continuous improvement. By understanding and embracing the importance of preparation, both NASCAR drivers and Christians can achieve their goals and navigate the challenges they face with confidence and determination. As 2 Timothy 2:15 reminds us, "Study to shew thyself approved unto God, a workman that needeth not to be ashamed, rightly dividing the word of truth."

Chapter 2 Endurance

Endurance is essential both in NASCAR racing and in the Christian life, as both require a great deal of stamina and perseverance to achieve their goals. In NASCAR, endurance is critical because races are long and demanding, often lasting several hours. Drivers must maintain their focus, concentration, and physical stamina throughout the race to navigate the high speeds, sharp turns, and intense competition. They must endure the physical strain of driving for extended periods, the mental challenge of staying sharp and making quick decisions, and the emotional pressure of competing against the best in the sport. Endurance training is a key part of a driver's preparation, involving physical fitness routines to build strength and stamina, as well as mental exercises to enhance concentration and resilience. Drivers must also manage the fatigue that sets in during a race, staying hydrated and maintaining their energy levels to ensure they can perform at their best until the very end.

Similarly, Christians are called to endure trials and remain faithful throughout their lives. The Christian journey is often described as a race, one that requires spiritual stamina and perseverance. Just as NASCAR drivers face challenges on the track, Christians encounter various trials and temptations in their walk of faith. These can include personal struggles, opposition from others, and internal doubts. Endurance in the Christian life means remaining steadfast in faith, even when circumstances are difficult. It involves trusting in God's promises and relying on His strength to get through tough times. James 1:12 highlights the importance of endurance, saying, "Blessed is the man that endureth temptation: for when he is tried, he shall receive the crown of life, which the Lord hath promised to them that love him." This verse reminds Christians that enduring trials leads to a reward—the crown of life that God has promised to those who love Him.

Just as a NASCAR driver prepares for endurance by building physical and mental strength, Christians prepare for spiritual endurance through practices like prayer, Bible study, and fellowship. Prayer helps Christians stay connected to God, seek His guidance, and find the strength to persevere. Bible study provides encouragement and wisdom from God's Word, offering examples of others who have endured trials and remained faithful. Fellowship with other believers provides support and encouragement, helping Christians stay strong in their faith. In NASCAR, teamwork also plays a crucial role in endurance. Drivers rely on their pit crews to make quick and efficient pit stops, ensuring the car remains in optimal condition throughout the race. Similarly, Christians rely on their spiritual community to support them, pray for them, and provide practical help during difficult times. This mutual support is vital for maintaining endurance in the race of faith.

Endurance in both NASCAR and the Christian life also involves a focus on the goal. In NASCAR, the goal is to reach the finish line and win the race. Drivers keep this goal in mind, pushing through fatigue and obstacles to achieve it. In the Christian life, the goal is to grow in faith, become more like Christ, and ultimately receive the eternal reward that God has promised. Keeping this goal in mind helps Christians persevere through trials, knowing that their efforts have a purpose and a reward. The Apostle Paul often used the metaphor of a race to describe the Christian life. In 1 Corinthians 9:24-27, he writes, "24 Know ye not that they which run in a race run all, but one receiveth the prize? So run, that ye may obtain. And every man that striveth for the mastery is temperate in all things. Now they do it to obtain a corruptible crown; but we an incorruptible. I therefore so run, not as uncertainly; so fight I, not as one that beateth the air: But I keep under my body, and bring it into subjection: lest that by any means, when I have preached to others, I myself should be a castaway." Paul emphasizes the importance of discipline and focus on the race of faith, encouraging believers to strive for the incorruptible crown that God promises.

Both NASCAR drivers and Christians must also learn to manage setbacks and failures. In a race, drivers may experience mechanical failures, crashes, or other issues that set them back. Endurance means not giving up when these setbacks occur but continuing to push forward and do their best. Similarly, Christians face setbacks in their spiritual journey, such as falling into sin, experiencing personal loss, or facing discouragement. Endurance in the Christian life means confessing sins, seeking God's forgiveness, and continuing to pursue a relationship with Him despite these setbacks. Hebrews 12:1-2 encourages believers to run the race with endurance, saying, "Wherefore seeing we also are compassed about with so great a cloud of witnesses, let us lay aside every weight, and the sin which doth so easily beset us, and let us run with patience the race that is set before us, Looking unto Jesus the author and finisher of our faith; who for the joy that was set before him endured the cross, despising the shame, and is set down at the right hand of the throne of God." This passage reminds Christians to look to Jesus as their example of endurance, knowing that He endured the ultimate trial for the joy set before Him.

Another aspect of endurance is learning to pace oneself. In a long NASCAR race, drivers must manage their speed and energy to avoid burning out too quickly. They need to know when to push hard and when to conserve energy. Similarly, Christians must learn to pace themselves in their spiritual journey. This involves balancing times of intense activity and service with times of rest and renewal. Jesus Himself often withdrew to solitary places to pray and rest, setting an example for His followers. Taking time for rest and spiritual renewal helps Christians maintain their endurance for the long journey of faith.

Both NASCAR drivers and Christians must also cultivate resilience. Resilience is the ability to bounce back from difficulties and continue moving forward. In NASCAR, resilience is crucial for recovering from crashes or mechanical issues and getting back into the race. For Christians, resilience means trusting in God's faithfulness and continuing to follow Him even when life is hard. Romans 5:3-5 speaks to the value of endurance and resilience, saying, "And not only so, but we glory in tribulations also: knowing that tribulation worketh patience; And patience, experience; and experience, hope: And hope maketh not ashamed; because the love of God is shed abroad in our hearts by the Holy Ghost which is given unto us." This passage highlights how enduring trials produces perseverance, character, and hope, ultimately strengthening a believer's faith.

Endurance in both NASCAR and the Christian life also involves a willingness to make sacrifices. NASCAR drivers often make significant sacrifices, such as time away from family and intense physical training, to succeed in their sport. Similarly, Christians are called to make sacrifices in their walk of faith. This can include giving up certain comforts or desires, serving others selflessly, and sometimes facing persecution for their beliefs. Jesus taught about the cost of discipleship in Luke 9:23, saying, " And he said to them all, If any man will come after me, let him deny himself, and take up his cross daily, and follow me." This verse emphasizes the daily commitment and sacrifice required to follow Christ faithfully.

Both NASCAR drivers and Christians also benefit from mentors and role models who can guide and inspire them. In NASCAR, young drivers often look up to experienced veterans who have demonstrated endurance and success in their careers. These mentors provide valuable advice, encouragement, and examples to follow. Similarly, Christians benefit from having spiritual mentors and role models who can offer guidance, support, and inspiration. Hebrews 13:7 encourages believers to remember and imitate their spiritual leaders, saying, " Remember them which have the rule over you, who have spoken unto you the word of God: whose faith follow, considering the end of their conversation."

Finally, endurance in both NASCAR and the Christian life involves a reliance on a higher power. NASCAR drivers rely on their teams, technology, and sometimes even a bit of luck to succeed. Christians, however, rely on God as their ultimate source of strength and guidance. Philippians 4:13 reminds believers, "I can do all things through Christ which strengtheneth me." This verse emphasizes that Christians do not endure trials and challenges on their own but through the strength and support that Christ provides.

In conclusion, endurance is a vital component of both NASCAR racing and the Christian life. NASCAR drivers prepare for endurance through physical training, mental exercises, teamwork, and strategic planning. Similarly, Christians prepare for spiritual endurance through prayer, Bible study, fellowship, and reliance on God. Endurance involves remaining steadfast in the face of challenges, managing setbacks, pacing oneself, cultivating resilience, making sacrifices, seeking guidance from mentors, and relying on a higher power. By embracing these principles, both NASCAR drivers and Christians can achieve their goals and navigate the challenges they face with confidence and determination. As James 1:12 reminds us, "Blessed is the man that endureth temptation: for when he is tried, he shall receive the crown of life, which the Lord hath promised to them that love him."

Chapter 3 Focus

Focus is crucial in both NASCAR and the Christian life, as staying focused on the right things can mean the difference between success and failure. In NASCAR, drivers must stay intensely focused on the track at all times. This focus helps them navigate high speeds, sharp turns, and the presence of other cars on the track. Losing concentration for even a split second can lead to mistakes, crashes, or losing the race. NASCAR drivers need to maintain their focus despite the noise of the crowd, the pressure of the competition, and the physical demands of driving. They must stay alert to changes in track conditions, weather, and the behavior of other drivers. This focus is supported by a team of spotters and crew members who provide crucial information and guidance throughout the race, helping the driver make split-second decisions and stay on the optimal path.

Similarly, Christians must keep their focus on Christ to navigate the challenges and distractions of life. The Bible encourages believers to fix their eyes on Jesus, as stated in Hebrews 12:2 "Looking unto Jesus the author and finisher of our faith; who for the joy that was set before him endured the cross, despising the shame, and is set down at the right hand of the throne of God." This verse reminds Christians that Jesus is both the beginning and the end of their faith journey. By keeping their focus on Him, they can endure the trials and temptations that come their way, just as Jesus endured the cross for the joy set before Him. Focusing on Christ means prioritizing a relationship with Him through prayer, reading the Bible, and seeking His guidance in all aspects of life. It involves turning away from distractions and temptations that can lead one off course and instead, staying committed to living according to His teachings and example.

In NASCAR, focus is not just about the immediate moment but also about the overall strategy for the race. Drivers and their teams plan extensively, considering factors such as pit stop timing, tire management, and fuel consumption. This strategic focus helps them make informed decisions that can lead to victory. Similarly, Christians need to focus on their long-term spiritual goals, such as growing in faith, serving others, and fulfilling God's purpose for their lives. This involves setting aside time for spiritual practices, such as prayer, worship, and studying the Bible, which help to keep their minds and hearts aligned with God's will. It also means being intentional about avoiding distractions that can pull them away from their faith, such as negative influences, unhealthy habits, or materialistic pursuits.

Both NASCAR drivers and Christians face numerous distractions that can threaten their focus. For a NASCAR driver, distractions can come in the form of mechanical issues, changing weather conditions, or aggressive maneuvers by other drivers. Maintaining focus in the face of these distractions is crucial for staying on track and reaching the finish line. Similarly, Christians face distractions that can draw them away from their faith, such as personal struggles, societal pressures, or the busyness of everyday life. Maintaining focus on Christ requires intentional effort and discipline. It means making choices that support one's faith and avoiding those that lead to spiritual drift. For example, spending time in prayer and Bible study each day helps to keep one's focus on Christ, while engaging in activities that are contrary to Christian values can lead to a loss of focus and spiritual disorientation.

Focus also involves perseverance in both NASCAR and the Christian life. In a race, drivers may encounter setbacks such as flat tires, collisions, or engine problems. Staying focused and persevering through these challenges is essential for making it to the finish line. Similarly, Christians may face trials and difficulties that test their faith and commitment. Persevering with a focus on Christ helps them navigate these challenges and grow stronger in their faith. James 1:2-4 encourages believers to "My brethren, count it all joy when ye fall into divers temptations; Knowing this, that the trying of your faith worketh patience. But let patience have her perfect work, that ye may be perfect and entire, wanting nothing." This passage reminds Christians that enduring trials with a focus on Christ leads to spiritual maturity and completeness.

Another important aspect of focus in NASCAR is the ability to stay calm under pressure. Drivers must maintain their composure even when things go wrong or when the competition is intense. This calm focus allows them to make rational decisions and avoid panic. Similarly, Christians are called to stay calm and trust in God, even when faced with difficult circumstances. Philippians 4:6-7 advises, "Be careful for nothing; but in every thing by prayer and supplication with thanksgiving let your requests be made known unto God. And the peace of God, which passeth all understanding, shall keep your hearts and minds through Christ Jesus." This verse encourages believers to focus on prayer and thanksgiving, trusting that God's peace will guard their hearts and minds.

In both NASCAR and the Christian life, focus also involves listening to guidance. NASCAR drivers rely on their spotters and crew chiefs to provide critical information and advice during the race. These team members help the driver navigate the track, avoid hazards, and make strategic decisions. Similarly, Christians rely on the guidance of the Holy Spirit, as well as the counsel of other believers, to stay on the right path. Proverbs 3:5-6 teaches, "Trust in the LORD with all thine heart; and lean not unto thine own understanding. In all thy ways acknowledge him, and he shall direct thy paths." By focusing on God's guidance and seeking wise counsel, Christians can navigate the complexities of life with confidence.

Focus on both NASCAR and the Christian life also requires self-discipline. NASCAR drivers must discipline themselves to maintain peak physical and mental condition, adhere to their race strategy, and avoid unnecessary risks. Similarly,

Christians must practice self-discipline to stay focused on their spiritual journey. This includes making time for prayer and Bible study, resisting temptation, and living according to God's commandments. 1 Corinthians 9:24-27 compares the Christian life to a race, urging believers to exercise self-discipline: "Know ye not that they which run in a race run all, but one receiveth the prize? So run, that ye may obtain. And every man that striveth for the mastery is temperate in all things. Now they do it to obtain a corruptible crown; but we an incorruptible. I therefore so run, not as uncertainly; so fight I, not as one that beateth the air: But I keep under my body, and bring it into subjection: lest that by any means, when I have preached to others, I myself should be a castaway."

Both NASCAR drivers and Christians must also learn to prioritize their focus. In a race, drivers prioritize their focus on the most important aspects, such as track conditions, their car's performance, and the actions of other drivers. They must ignore less important distractions and stay concentrated on what matters most. Similarly, Christians must prioritize their focus on their relationship with Christ and living out their faith. This may involve making difficult choices about how to spend their time and energy, ensuring that their primary focus remains on their spiritual growth and service to God and others. Matthew 6:33 encourages believers to prioritize their focus on God's kingdom: "But seek ye first the kingdom of God, and his righteousness; and all these things shall be added unto you."

Focus on both NASCAR and the Christian life also involves a clear vision of the goal. For NASCAR drivers, the goal is to finish the race and achieve the best possible position. This vision keeps them motivated and focused throughout the race. For Christians, the ultimate goal is to grow in their relationship with Christ, become more like Him, and eventually receive the eternal reward of being with Him in heaven. Keeping this vision in mind helps Christians stay focused on their spiritual journey, even when the path is difficult. Philippians 3:13-14 captures this focus on the goal: "Brethren, I count not myself to have apprehended: but this one thing I do, forgetting those things which are behind, and reaching forth unto those things which are before, I press toward the mark for the prize of the high calling of God in

Christ Jesus."

In both scenarios, maintaining focus also involves setting aside time for preparation and reflection. NASCAR drivers spend significant time preparing for races through practice sessions, strategy meetings, and reviewing past performances. Similarly, Christians benefit from setting aside time for spiritual preparation and reflection. This includes regular prayer, Bible study, and quiet time to reflect on God's Word and listen for His guidance. These practices help

Christians maintain their focus on Christ and ensure that their lives are aligned with His will. Psalm 46:10 encourages believers to take time for reflection: "Be still, and know that I am God: I will be exalted among the heathen, I will be exalted in the earth."

Both NASCAR drivers and Christians also learn to develop a laser-like focus in the midst of chaos. During a race, the track can become chaotic with crashes, mechanical failures, and intense competition. Drivers must block out the chaos and stay focused on their driving. Similarly, life can become chaotic with various challenges and distractions. Christians must learn to block out the chaos and maintain their focus on Christ. This requires developing a strong inner focus and reliance on God's strength and peace. Isaiah 26:3 promises peace to those who stay focused on God: "Thou wilt keep him in perfect peace, whose mind is stayed on thee: because he trusteth in thee."

Another important aspect of focus is the ability to adapt and adjust. NASCAR drivers must be able to adapt to changing track conditions, weather, and the behavior of other drivers.

This adaptability helps them maintain their focus and perform well under varying circumstances. Similarly, Christians must be able to adapt to changing life circumstances while keeping their focus on Christ. This involves trusting in God's plan and being willing to adjust one's plans and expectations in response to His leading. Proverbs 16:9 reminds believers of the importance of trusting in God's guidance: "A man's heart deviseth his way: but the

LORD directeth his steps."

In conclusion, focus is a vital component of both NASCAR racing and the Christian life. NASCAR drivers must stay focused on the track, maintain their concentration, and navigate distractions and challenges to succeed in the race. Similarly, Christians must keep their focus on Christ, prioritizing their relationship with Him and living according to His teachings. This involves prayer, Bible study, fellowship, self-discipline, and reliance on God's guidance. By maintaining a clear vision of their spiritual goals, setting aside time for preparation and reflection, and developing a strong inner focus, Christians can navigate the challenges of life with confidence and determination. As Hebrews 12:2 reminds us, "Looking unto Jesus the author and finisher of our faith; who for the joy that was set before him endured the cross, despising the shame, and is set down at the right hand of the throne of God."

Chapter 4 Teamwork

Teamwork is essential in both NASCAR and the Christian life because success in both areas depends on people working together effectively. In NASCAR, the driver's performance on the track is just one part of the equation. Behind the scenes, a whole team of people works together to ensure that the car is in top condition and that the race strategy is sound. This team includes the pit crew, engineers, mechanics, and spotters, all playing crucial roles. The pit crew performs lightning-fast tire changes, refuels the car, and makes necessary adjustments during pit stops. Their speed and precision can make the difference between winning and losing a race. Engineers and mechanics work tirelessly to finetune the car, ensuring that it performs optimally and handles the rigors of the race. Spotters provide the driver with vital information about the track, helping them navigate traffic and avoid potential hazards. The teamwork and coordination of all these individuals enable the driver to focus on driving and perform at their best. Similarly, in the Christian life, the body of Christ—also known as the Church—works together in unity. Just as a NASCAR team consists of many members with different roles, the body of Christ is made up of many members, each with unique gifts and functions. 1 Corinthians 12:12 states, "For as the body is one, and hath many members, and all the members of that one body, being many, are one body: so also is Christ." This verse highlights the importance of unity and collaboration among believers. Each member of the body of Christ has a specific role to play, and their combined efforts contribute to the health and growth of the Church. Some members are gifted in teaching, others in serving, some in encouraging, and others in leadership. When each person uses their gifts and works together with others, the Church functions effectively and can accomplish its mission of spreading the Gospel and serving the community.

In both NASCAR and the Christian life, communication is key to effective teamwork. NASCAR teams rely on constant communication between the driver, the pit crew, and the spotters. During a race, the driver receives updates and instructions through a headset, allowing them to make informed decisions and adjustments. This communication ensures that everyone is on the same page and can respond quickly to changing conditions. Similarly, in the body of Christ, communication is vital. Believers are encouraged to speak the truth in love, offer encouragement, and support one another. Open and honest communication helps build trust and fosters a sense of unity and cooperation. Ephesians 4:15-16 emphasizes the importance of communication and working together: " But speaking the truth in love, may grow up into him in all things, which is the head, even Christ: From whom the whole body fitly joined together and compacted by that which every joint supplieth, according to the effectual working in the measure of every part, maketh increase of the body unto the edifying of itself in love."

Another crucial aspect of teamwork is mutual support and encouragement. In NASCAR, team members support each other by providing the resources and assistance needed for success. The driver relies on the pit crew for quick and efficient service, while the pit crew depends on the driver to execute their strategy on the track. This mutual support creates a strong team dynamic and contributes to overall success. Similarly, in the Christian life, believers are called to support and encourage one another. Hebrews 10:24-25 encourages believers to " And let us consider one another to provoke unto love and to good works: Not forsaking the assembling of ourselves together, as the manner of some is; but exhorting one another: and so much the more, as ye see the day approaching." By supporting one another through prayer, encouragement, and practical help, believers strengthen the body of Christ and help each other grow in faith.

Trust is another essential component of teamwork in both NASCAR and the Christian life. In NASCAR, the driver must trust the pit crew to perform their tasks quickly and accurately, while the pit crew must trust the driver to follow the race strategy and make smart decisions on the track. This trust is built through practice, experience, and a shared commitment to the team's goals. Similarly, in the body of Christ, trust is crucial. Believers must trust one another to use their gifts and fulfill their roles effectively. This trust is built through shared experiences, mutual accountability, and a commitment to the common goal of glorifying God and advancing His kingdom. Proverbs 3:5-6 encourages believers with "And let us consider one another to provoke unto love and to good works: Not forsaking the assembling of ourselves together, as the manner of some is; but exhorting one another: and so much the more, as ye see the day approaching."

In both NASCAR and the Christian life, everyone has a role to play, and each role is important. In NASCAR, the driver gets most of the attention, but without the support of the pit crew, engineers, and other team members, the driver could not succeed. Each member's contribution is vital to the team's overall performance. Similarly, in the body of Christ, each member's gifts and contributions are important. Romans 12:4-6a explains, "For as we have many members in one body, and all members have not the same office: So we, being many, are one body in Christ, and every one members one of another. Having then gifts differing according to the grace that is given to us, whether prophecy, let us prophesy according to the proportion of faith;". This passage emphasizes that every believer has a unique role and that all roles are necessary for the body to function effectively.

Teamwork also involves recognizing and valuing the diversity of gifts and abilities. In NASCAR, team members bring different skills and expertise to the table. The driver must have exceptional driving skills, the pit crew must be quick and precise, and the engineers must have technical knowledge. This diversity of skills allows the team to handle various challenges and perform at a high level. Similarly, the body of Christ is made up of individuals with diverse gifts and abilities. Some are gifted in teaching, others in hospitality, some in administration, and others in evangelism. This diversity of gifts allows the Church to meet different needs and serve the community effectively. 1 Peter 4:10-11 encourages believers to use their gifts to serve others: "As every man hath received the gift, even so minister the same one to another, as good stewards of the manifold grace of God. If any man speak, let him speak as the oracles of God; if any man minister, let him do it as of the ability which God giveth: that God in all things may be glorified through Jesus Christ, to whom be praise and dominion for ever and ever. Amen."

In NASCAR, teamwork requires coordination and cooperation. The pit crew must work together seamlessly, with each member performing their task quickly and accurately. The driver must cooperate with the team's strategy and follow the instructions provided by the spotters and crew chief. This coordination and cooperation are essential for success. Similarly, in the body of Christ, coordination and cooperation are crucial. Believers must work together, supporting one another and aligning their efforts to achieve common goals. Ephesians 4:3-4 encourages believers to "Endeavouring to keep the unity of the Spirit in the bond of peace. There is one body, and one Spirit, even as ye are called in one hope of your calling;" By working together in unity, believers can accomplish more and reflect God's love and grace to the world.

Both NASCAR teams and the body of Christ face challenges that require perseverance and resilience. In NASCAR, teams may encounter mechanical failures, accidents, or other setbacks during a race. Perseverance and resilience help the team overcome these challenges and continue striving for success. Similarly, the body of Christ faces challenges such as persecution, internal conflicts, and external opposition. Perseverance and resilience are essential for overcoming these challenges and remaining faithful to God's calling. Galatians 6:9 encourages believers to persevere: "And let us not be weary in well doing: for in due season we shall reap, if we faint not."

Leadership is another important aspect of teamwork in both NASCAR and the Christian life. In NASCAR, the crew chief provides leadership, making strategic decisions and guiding the team. The driver also provides leadership on the track, executing the race strategy and making quick decisions. Effective leadership helps the team stay focused, motivated, and coordinated. Similarly, in the body of Christ, leadership is important. Church leaders, such as pastors and elders, provide guidance, teaching, and support to the congregation. Effective leadership helps the Church stay focused on its mission and encourages spiritual growth. Hebrews 13:17 advises believers to respect and follow their leaders: " Obey them that have the rule over you, and submit yourselves: for they watch for your souls, as they that must give account, that they may do it with joy, and not with grief: for that is unprofitable for you."

Accountability is also crucial for effective teamwork. In NASCAR, team members hold each other accountable for their performance and responsibilities. This accountability ensures that everyone is doing their part and contributing to the team's success. Similarly, in the body of Christ, accountability helps believers stay on track and grow in their faith. By holding one another accountable, believers can encourage each other to live according to God's Word and fulfill their roles in the Church. James 5:16 emphasizes the importance of accountability: "Confess your faults one to another, and pray one for another, that ye may be healed. The effectual fervent prayer of a righteous man availeth much."

In both NASCAR and the Christian life, teamwork also involves celebrating successes and learning from failures. In NASCAR, teams celebrate victories together, recognizing the contributions of each member. They also review and learn from their performance, identifying areas for improvement. Similarly, in the body of Christ, believers celebrate spiritual victories, such as new believers coming to faith or successful ministry efforts. They also learn from their experiences, seeking God's guidance for growth and improvement. Romans 12:15 encourages believers to " Rejoice with them that do rejoice, and weep with them that weep," highlighting the importance of sharing both joys and sorrows within the community.

Both NASCAR teams and the body of Christ benefit from a shared vision and mission. In NASCAR, the shared vision is to win races and championships. This vision motivates and unites the team, giving them a common goal to strive toward. Similarly, the body of Christ shares the vision of spreading the Gospel and making disciples of all nations. This shared mission unites believers and gives them a common purpose. Matthew 28:19-20, known as the Great Commission, outlines this mission: " Go ye therefore, and teach all nations, baptizing them in the name of the Father, and of the Son, and of the Holy Ghost: Teaching them to observe all things whatsoever I have commanded you: and, lo, I am with you always, even unto the end of the world. Amen." By working together toward this shared mission, the body of Christ can have a greater impact on the world.

In both NASCAR and the Christian life, teamwork involves humility and a willingness to serve others. In NASCAR, team members often put the needs of the team above their own, working selflessly to support the driver and contribute to the team's success. Similarly, in the body of Christ, believers are called to serve one another in humility. Philippians 2:3-4 encourages believers to " Let nothing be done through strife or vainglory; but in lowliness of mind let each esteem other better than themselves. Look not every man on his own things, but every man also on the things of others." By serving one another with humility, believers reflect Christ's love and build up the body of Christ.

Both NASCAR teams and the body of Christ rely on the strengths and contributions of each member. In NASCAR, the team's success depends on each member performing their role to the best of their ability. The driver relies on the pit crew, engineers, and other team members to support them and ensure the car performs optimally. Similarly, in the body of Christ, each member's strengths and contributions are vital to the overall health and growth of the Church. When believers use their gifts and abilities to serve others, the body of Christ is strengthened and equipped to fulfill its mission. 1 Corinthians 12:18-20 emphasizes the importance of each member's contributions: "But now hath God set the members every one of them in the body, as it hath pleased him. And if they were all one member, where were the body? But now are they many members, yet but one body."

Teamwork in both NASCAR and the Christian life also involves a commitment to growth and improvement. In NASCAR, teams constantly seek ways to improve their performance, whether through better technology, more efficient pit stops, or improved driving techniques. This commitment to growth helps them stay competitive and achieve success. Similarly, in the body of Christ, believers are called to grow in their faith and become more like Christ. This involves a commitment to spiritual disciplines, such as prayer, Bible study, and fellowship, as well as a willingness to learn and grow from experiences. Ephesians 4:15 encourages believers by stating "But speaking the truth in love, may grow up into him in all things, which is the head, even Christ:"

In both NASCAR and the Christian life, teamwork involves perseverance and resilience in the face of challenges. NASCAR teams face various challenges during races, such as mechanical failures, accidents, or difficult track conditions. Perseverance and resilience help the team overcome these challenges and continue striving for success. Similarly, the body of Christ faces challenges such as persecution, internal conflicts, and external opposition. Perseverance and resilience are essential for overcoming these challenges and remaining faithful to God's calling. James 1:2-4 encourages believers with "My brethren, count it all joy when ye fall into divers temptations; Knowing this, that the trying of your faith worketh patience. But let patience have her perfect work, that ye may be perfect and entire, wanting nothing."

In conclusion, teamwork is a vital component of both NASCAR racing and the Christian life. NASCAR drivers depend on their team, including the pit crew, engineers, mechanics, and spotters, to achieve success on the track. Similarly, the body of Christ works together in unity, with each member using their unique gifts and abilities to contribute to the health and growth of the Church. Effective teamwork in both areas involves communication, mutual support, trust, recognizing and valuing diversity, coordination, perseverance, leadership, accountability, celebrating successes, and learning from failures. By working together in unity and focusing on their shared mission, both NASCAR teams and the body of Christ can achieve their goals and make a positive impact on the world. As 1 Corinthians 12:12 reminds us, "My brethren, count it all joy when ye fall into divers temptations; Knowing this, that the trying of your faith worketh patience. But let patience have her perfect work, that ye may be perfect and entire, wanting nothing."

Chapter 5 Obedience

Obedience is crucial in both NASCAR and the Christian life because following rules and regulations is essential for success and harmony. In NASCAR, drivers must obey a strict set of rules and regulations to ensure safety, fairness, and the smooth running of the race. These rules govern everything from the technical specifications of the cars to how drivers conduct themselves on the track. Drivers must follow speed limits in the pit lane, avoid dangerous maneuvers, and adhere to guidelines about overtaking and blocking. There are also rules about when and how to make pit stops, and penalties for infractions like jumping the start or causing collisions. These rules are enforced by officials who monitor the race and issue penalties for violations. Obedience to these rules is essential because it ensures a level playing field and helps prevent accidents. A driver who disobeys the rules not only risks penalties but also endangers themselves and others. Similarly, Christians are called to follow God's commandments, which are laid out in the Bible. These commandments serve as guidelines for living a life that is pleasing to God and beneficial to others. Jesus emphasized the importance of obedience in John 14:15, saying, "If ye love me, keep my commandments." This verse highlights that obedience to God's commandments is a way of showing love and devotion to Him.

Just as NASCAR drivers must obey the rules of the race, Christians must obey God's commandments in their daily lives. God's commandments cover various aspects of life, including how we treat others, how we conduct ourselves, and how we worship Him. The Ten Commandments, for example, provide fundamental principles for living a moral and righteous life. These include honoring one's parents, refraining from stealing and lying, and keeping the Sabbath day holy. Mark 12:30-31 teaches "And thou shalt love the Lord thy God with all thy heart, and with all thy soul, and with all thy mind, and with all thy strength: this is the first commandment. And the second is like, namely this, Thou shalt love thy neighbour as thyself. There is none other commandment greater than these." Obedience to these commandments is essential for maintaining a close relationship with God and living in harmony with others.

In both NASCAR and the Christian life, obedience requires discipline and self-control. NASCAR drivers must discipline themselves to follow the rules, even when it is tempting to cut corners or take risks for a competitive advantage. They must exercise self-control to avoid actions that could lead to penalties or accidents. Similarly, Christians must discipline themselves to obey God's commandments, even when it is difficult or inconvenient. This requires self-control to resist temptations and make choices that align with God's will. Galatians 5:22-23 lists self-control as one of the fruits of the Spirit, emphasizing its importance in the Christian life.

Obedience in NASCAR also involves respect for authority. Drivers must respect the officials who enforce the rules and make decisions about penalties. They must accept the authority of race stewards and comply with their rulings, even if they disagree. This respect for authority helps maintain order and fairness in the sport. Similarly, Christians are called to respect God's authority and submit to His will. This means trusting that God's commandments are for our good and obeying them out of reverence for Him. James 4:7 encourages believers to "Submit yourselves therefore to God. Resist the devil, and he will flee from you." Submission to God's authority is a sign of humility and trust in His wisdom.

In both NASCAR and the Christian life, obedience leads to rewards. In NASCAR, drivers who obey the rules and perform well on the track can achieve success, win races, and earn championships. Their obedience to the rules helps them avoid penalties that could hinder their performance and allows them to compete fairly. Similarly, Christians who obey God's commandments can experience the blessings of a close relationship with Him, spiritual growth, and eternal life. Jesus promised rewards for obedience, saying in John 14:21, "He that hath my commandments, and keepeth them, he it is that loveth me: and he that loveth me shall be loved of my Father, and I will love him, and will manifest myself to him." Obedience to God's commandments brings us closer to Him and allows us to experience His love and presence in our lives.

Obedience also involves accountability. In NASCAR, drivers are held accountable for their actions on the track. If they break the rules, they face penalties such as time deductions, fines, or disqualification. This accountability helps ensure that all drivers adhere to the same standards and that the competition is fair. Similarly, Christians are accountable to God for their actions. The Bible teaches that we will all stand before God and give an account of our lives (Romans 14:12). This accountability encourages believers to live in obedience to God's commandments and to strive for righteousness.

In both NASCAR and the Christian life, obedience fosters a sense of community and cooperation. NASCAR teams work together to achieve success, and this requires all members to obey the rules and work towards common goals. When drivers and teams obey the rules, it creates an environment of trust and respect, allowing everyone to focus on racing and teamwork. Similarly, obedience to God's commandments fosters unity and cooperation within the body of Christ. When believers obey God's commands to love one another, serve each other, and live in harmony, it strengthens the church community and allows it to function effectively. Ephesians 4:3-4 encourages believers to " Endeavouring to keep the unity of the Spirit in the bond of peace. There is one body, and one Spirit, even as ye are called in one hope of your calling." Obedience to God's commandments helps create a loving and supportive community where believers can grow in faith and support one another.

Obedience in both NASCAR and the Christian life also requires perseverance. NASCAR drivers must consistently obey the rules throughout the entire race, not just at the beginning or end. This requires endurance and a commitment to following the rules, even when the race is long and challenging. Similarly, Christians must persevere in their obedience to God's commandments throughout their lives. This involves staying faithful and committed to God's will, even when faced with trials, temptations, and challenges. Hebrews 10:36 encourages believers to persevere: "For ye have need of patience, that, after ye have done the will of God, ye might receive the promise." Perseverance in obedience leads to spiritual growth and the fulfillment of God's promises.

In both NASCAR and the Christian life, obedience is a sign of love and loyalty. NASCAR drivers demonstrate their commitment to the sport and their respect for the rules by obeying them. This obedience shows their dedication to fair competition and their loyalty to their team and fans. Similarly, Christians demonstrate their love for God and their loyalty to Him by obeying His commandments. Jesus said in John 14:15, "If ye love me, keep my commandments." Obedience is an expression of our love for God and our desire to honor Him with our lives.

Both NASCAR drivers and Christians face challenges that test their obedience. In NASCAR, drivers may be tempted to bend the rules to gain a competitive edge or may face situations where following the rules is difficult. Similarly, Christians face temptations and trials that challenge their commitment to obeying God's commandments. In both cases, staying true to the rules and commandments requires strength, integrity, and a firm commitment to doing what is right. 1 Corinthians 10:13 offers encouragement to believers facing temptation: "There hath no temptation taken you, but such as is common to man: but God is faithful, who will not suffer you to be tempted above that ye are able; but will with the temptation also make a way to escape, that ye may be able to bear it." God's faithfulness provides the strength and support needed to remain obedient in difficult times.

Obedience in both NASCAR and the Christian life involves learning and growth. NASCAR drivers continually learn and improve their skills, and part of this learning process involves understanding and adhering to the rules. By obeying the rules, drivers gain experience, learn from their mistakes, and become better competitors. Similarly, Christians grow in their faith and understanding of God's will by obeying His commandments. Obedience helps believers learn more about God's character, His plans, and how to live a life that pleases Him. 2 Timothy 3:16-17 highlights the importance of God's

Word in this process: "All scripture is given by inspiration of God, and is profitable for doctrine, for reproof, for correction, for instruction in righteousness: That the man of God may be perfect, thoroughly furnished unto all good works." Studying and obeying God's Word helps believers grow in righteousness and equips them for every good work.

Obedience also brings peace and stability. In NASCAR, when drivers obey the rules, it creates a predictable and fair environment where everyone knows what to expect. This stability allows drivers to focus on their performance and compete fairly. Similarly, in the Christian life, obedience to God's commandments brings peace and stability. God's commandments provide clear guidance for how to live, make decisions, and relate to others. This guidance helps believers navigate life's challenges and uncertainties with confidence and peace. Psalm 119:165 says, "Great peace have they which love thy law: and nothing shall offend them." Obedience to God's law brings peace and security.

In both NASCAR and the Christian life, obedience is a journey, not a one-time event. NASCAR drivers must continually obey the rules throughout their careers, adapting to new regulations and learning from their experiences. Similarly, Christians must continually strive to obey God's commandments, growing in their faith and understanding over time. This journey of obedience involves daily decisions to follow God's will and align one's life with His teachings. It requires ongoing commitment and a willingness to learn and grow. Philippians 3:12-14 captures this journey of obedience: "Not as though I had already attained, either were already perfect: but I follow after, if that I may apprehend that for which also I am apprehended of Christ Jesus. Brethren, I count not myself to have apprehended: but this one thing I

do, forgetting those things which are behind, and reaching forth unto those things which are before, I press toward the mark for the prize of the high calling of God in Christ Jesus."

Both NASCAR drivers and Christians are examples to others through their obedience. NASCAR drivers who consistently obey the rules and demonstrate good sportsmanship set a positive example for other drivers and fans. Their obedience inspires others to follow the rules and compete fairly. Similarly, Christians who obey God's commandments set an example for others to follow. Their obedience and commitment to God's will serve as a testimony of their faith and can inspire others to seek a relationship with God. Matthew 5:16 encourages believers to let their light shine before others: "Let your light so shine before men, that they may see your good works, and glorify your Father which is in heaven." Obedience to God's commandments allows believers to be a light in the world and bring glory to God.

In conclusion, obedience is a vital component of both NASCAR racing and the Christian life. NASCAR drivers must obey a strict set of rules and regulations to ensure safety, fairness, and the smooth running of the race. Similarly, Christians are called to follow God's commandments, which serve as guidelines for living a life that is pleasing to God and beneficial to others. Obedience in both areas requires discipline, self-control, respect for authority, perseverance, and a commitment to learning and growth. It fosters a sense of community and cooperation, brings peace and stability, and serves as an example to others. By obeying the rules and commandments, both NASCAR drivers and Christians can achieve success, experience rewards, and live in harmony with others. As John 14:15 reminds us, obedience is an expression of our love for God: "If ye love me, keep my commandments." Through obedience, we show our devotion to God and our desire to honor Him with our lives.

Chapter 6 Pit Stops

Pit stops are crucial in NASCAR, just as times of rest and renewal are essential in the Christian life. In NASCAR, pit stops are brief but vital breaks during a race where the car is refueled, tires are changed, and necessary adjustments are made to ensure the vehicle performs optimally. These stops are meticulously planned and executed with precision by the pit crew to minimize time lost and maximize performance. The driver pulls into the pit, and within seconds, the team jumps into action, changing tires, refueling, and making any necessary mechanical adjustments. This teamwork and efficiency can be the difference between winning and losing the race. Pit stops allow the car to continue racing at its best, prevent mechanical failures, and ensure the driver has the best possible chance of success.

Similarly, Christians need regular times of rest and renewal in God's presence to maintain their spiritual health and effectiveness. Just as a car cannot run indefinitely without refueling and maintenance, people cannot continue to function effectively without taking time to rest and renew their spirits. These spiritual "pit stops" involve setting aside time to be with God, seeking His presence, and allowing Him to refresh and strengthen us. Matthew 11:28 says, "Come unto me, all ye that labour and are heavy laden, and I will give you rest." This verse highlights the invitation from Jesus to find rest in Him. Just as the car must stop for maintenance, Christians must pause from their busy lives to spend time with God, pray, read the Bible, and reflect on His goodness and guidance.

In NASCAR, pit stops are not just about maintaining the car's physical condition but also about making strategic adjustments. The pit crew may tweak the car's setup to better suit the track conditions or the driver's needs, improving its performance for the remainder of the race. Similarly, in the Christian life, times of rest and renewal are opportunities for

God to make necessary adjustments in our hearts and minds.

During these times, God can speak to us, provide clarity, and help us realign our priorities according to His will. It is during these moments of quiet reflection and prayer that we can hear God's voice more clearly and gain insight into His plans for our lives.

The efficiency and speed of a NASCAR pit stop are crucial, but the quality of the work done during this time is equally important. If the pit crew rushes and makes mistakes, it can lead to bigger problems down the line, such as mechanical failures or accidents. Therefore, they must balance speed with precision, ensuring that every task is performed correctly. Similarly, in the Christian life, while it is important to regularly take time for rest and renewal, the quality of this time is also vital. Simply going through the motions of prayer or Bible reading without genuine engagement and reflection can leave us spiritually unfulfilled. We must be intentional about seeking God with our whole hearts, genuinely desiring to connect with Him and receive His guidance and strength.

Pit stops in NASCAR also provide a moment for the driver to reset mentally. Racing is intense and demanding, requiring constant focus and quick decision-making. A pit stop offers a brief respite where the driver can catch their breath, refocus, and mentally prepare for the next segment of the race. Similarly, times of rest and renewal in the Christian life provide an opportunity to reset our minds and spirits. Life can be overwhelming, with numerous responsibilities, challenges, and distractions that can wear us down. Taking time to rest in God's presence allows us to cast our burdens on Him, find peace, and regain our spiritual focus. Philippians 4:6-7 reminds us, "Be careful for nothing; but in every thing by prayer and supplication with thanksgiving let your requests be made known unto God. And the peace of God, which passeth all understanding, shall keep your hearts and minds through Christ Jesus." This peace that comes from spending time with God helps us face life's challenges with renewed strength and clarity.

In NASCAR, pit stops are strategically timed to maximize their benefit while minimizing the time lost. Teams plan their stops based on factors like fuel levels, tire wear, and race conditions, ensuring they make the most of each opportunity. Similarly, Christians must be intentional about planning regular times for spiritual renewal. Just as a car needs regular maintenance, our spirits need consistent care and attention. This might involve setting aside daily time for prayer and Bible study, participating in weekly worship services, and taking occasional retreats for deeper reflection and connection with God. By intentionally planning these times, we ensure that we remain spiritually healthy and strong, ready to face whatever challenges come our way.

Another important aspect of pit stops in NASCAR is the role of the pit crew. The driver relies on the expertise and support of their team to make the necessary adjustments and keep the car in optimal condition. This teamwork is essential for success. Similarly, in the Christian life, we need the support and encouragement of our spiritual community. Fellow believers can provide prayer, guidance, and encouragement, helping us stay strong in our faith and navigate the challenges of life. Hebrews 10:24-25 encourages us to support one another: "And let us consider one another to provoke unto love and to good works: Not forsaking the assembling of ourselves together, as the manner of some is; but exhorting one another: and so much the more, as ye see the day approaching." Being part of a supportive Bible believing church helps us stay accountable and encouraged in the Lord.

Pit stops also highlight the importance of trust in both NASCAR and the Christian life. The driver must trust the pit crew to perform their tasks efficiently and correctly, knowing that their expertise is crucial for the race's success. Similarly, Christians must trust God to provide the rest and renewal we need. This trust involves surrendering our worries, burdens, and control to Him, believing that He will take care of us.

Proverbs 3:5-6 encourages us to trust in God's plan: "Trust in the LORD with all thine heart; and lean not unto thine own understanding. In all thy ways acknowledge him, and he shall direct thy paths." Trusting God allows us to rest in His presence, knowing that He will guide and strengthen us.

Just as a car needs regular pit stops to avoid breakdowns, Christians need regular times of rest and renewal to avoid spiritual burnout. Without these times, we can become weary, overwhelmed, and disconnected from God. Taking intentional breaks to rest in God's presence helps us recharge and prevents burnout. Isaiah 40:31 promises renewed strength to those who wait on the Lord: "But they that wait upon the LORD shall renew their strength; they shall mount up with wings as eagles; they shall run, and not be weary; and they shall walk, and not faint." By taking time to rest in God, we receive the strength we need to continue our journey with endurance and joy.

The benefit of pit stops extend beyond the immediate race. Regular maintenance and adjustments help ensure the car's longevity and performance in future races. Similarly, regular times of spiritual renewal have long-term benefits for our Christian walk. These times help us grow closer to God, deepen our faith, and develop a more intimate relationship with Him. They also equip us with the wisdom and strength we need to navigate life's challenges and fulfill God's purpose for our lives. Psalm 46:10 encourages us to be still and know that God is in control: "Be still, and know that I am God: I will be exalted among the heathen, I will be exalted in the earth." Taking time to rest in God's presence allows us to experience His peace and presence in deeper ways.

In NASCAR, pit stops are a team effort, requiring coordination and cooperation among the pit crew members. Each member has a specific role and responsibility, and their combined efforts ensure the car is ready to continue the race. Similarly, in the Christian life, we are part of the body of Christ, and our times of rest and renewal can involve the support and encouragement of others. Sharing our burdens, praying for one another, and seeking guidance from trusted mentors and friends are ways we can experience God's renewal together. Galatians 6:2 encourages us to bear one another's burdens: "Bear ye one another's burdens, and so fulfil the law of Christ." By supporting each other, we can experience God's renewal and strength in community.

Both NASCAR and the Christian life require a balance between action and rest. In NASCAR, the driver spends most of the time racing but must take necessary breaks for maintenance. Similarly, Christians are called to actively live out their faith, serving others, sharing the Gospel, and fulfilling God's purpose. However, to sustain this active life, we must also take regular times of rest and renewal. Jesus Himself modeled this balance, as He often withdrew to solitary places to pray and rest, even amid His busy ministry. Mark 1:35 describes one such instance: "And in the morning, rising up a great while before day, he went out, and departed into a solitary place, and there prayed." Following Jesus' example, we can find strength and renewal by regularly spending time in God's presence.

In NASCAR, pit stops also serve as an opportunity to address any issues or potential problems before they become major obstacles. Similarly, times of spiritual renewal allow us to address any issues or struggles we may be facing in our Christian walk. These times provide an opportunity to confess sins, seek forgiveness, and receive God's grace and healing. 1 John 1:9 assures us of God's forgiveness: "If we confess our sins, he is faithful and just to forgive us our sins, and to cleanse us from all unrighteousness." By taking time to address these issues in God's presence, we can experience His forgiveness and healing, allowing us to move forward with renewed strength and joy.

Just as pit stops are a regular part of a NASCAR race, times of rest and renewal should be a regular part of the Christian life. These times help us stay connected to God, maintain our spiritual health, and ensure that we are equipped to fulfill His purpose for our lives. By intentionally planning and prioritizing these times, we can experience

the abundant life that Jesus promised. John 10:10 says, "The thief cometh not, but for to steal, and to kill, and to destroy: I am come that they might have life, and that they might have it more abundantly." Taking time to rest in God's presence allows us to experience this abundant life and be a light to those around us.

In conclusion, pit stops are a vital component of both NASCAR racing and the Christian life. In NASCAR, pit stops provide necessary refueling, tire changes, and adjustments that ensure the car performs optimally and the driver has the best chance of success. Similarly, Christians need regular times of rest and renewal in God's presence to maintain their spiritual health and effectiveness. These times allow us to refuel spiritually, make necessary adjustments, and find rest in God's presence. Matthew 11:28 invites us to find rest in Jesus: "Come unto me, all ye that labour and are heavy laden, and I will give you rest." By taking these spiritual "pit stops," we can experience God's peace, strength, and renewal, allowing us to continue our journey with joy and purpose. Just as a car needs regular maintenance to avoid breakdowns, we need regular times of rest and renewal to avoid spiritual burnout. Through these times, we can experience His presence, receive His guidance, and grow in our faith, ultimately fulfilling His purpose for our lives and bringing glory to His name.

Chapter 7 Race Strategy

In NASCAR, having a solid race strategy is crucial for drivers who want to win. They can't just drive fast; they need a detailed plan that includes when to make pit stops, how to conserve fuel and tires, and how to react to different track conditions and other drivers' moves. This strategy involves the whole team, including the crew chief, engineers, and spotters, who provide constant updates and advice throughout the race. For example, if a driver is in the lead, they might decide to drive more conservatively to avoid mistakes, but if they are behind, they might take more risks to catch up. This kind of planning requires a lot of preparation, including studying previous races, practicing on the track, and fine-tuning the car. The driver and team must trust each other and communicate effectively to execute the plan successfully. Similarly, in the Christian life, believers are called to live with purpose and plan according to God's will. Just as a driver cannot win a race without a strategy, Christians cannot live a fulfilling life without seeking God's guidance and planning their lives according to His will. Proverbs 3:5-6 says, "Trust in the LORD with all thine heart; and lean not unto thine own understanding. In all thy ways acknowledge him, and he shall direct thy paths." This verse emphasizes the importance of trusting God and seeking His direction in every aspect of life.

Living with a purpose and plan according to God's will means recognizing that our lives are part of a bigger picture. Just as a NASCAR driver has a clear goal of winning the race, Christians have the ultimate goal of glorifying God and fulfilling His purposes. This involves seeking God's guidance through prayer, reading the Bible, and being open to the leading of the Holy Spirit. When Christians align their plans with God's will, they can navigate life's challenges and opportunities with confidence and clarity. Just as a driver trusts their crew chief and team, Christians trust the Lord to guide them on the right path.

In NASCAR, a race strategy includes making crucial decisions about when to push hard and when to hold back. Drivers need to know when to accelerate and take risks, and when to conserve fuel and tires. Similarly, in the Christian life, there are times to step out in faith and take bold actions, and times to wait patiently for God's timing. Ecclesiastes 3:1 reminds us, "To every thing there is a season, and a time to every purpose under the heaven." Understanding God's timing and being sensitive to His guidance helps Christians make wise decisions and avoid unnecessary pitfalls.

Just as a NASCAR driver must be flexible and adapt their strategy based on changing conditions, Christians must also be adaptable and willing to adjust their plans as God directs. Life is full of unexpected twists and turns, and a rigid plan that doesn't allow for change can lead to frustration and missed opportunities. Proverbs 16:9 says, "A man's heart deviseth his way: but the LORD directeth his steps." This means that while it is good to have plans, we must always be open to God's leading and ready to adjust our course as He directs.

A critical aspect of a race strategy in NASCAR is understanding the competition. Drivers study their opponents' strengths and weaknesses to develop a plan that gives them the best chance of winning. In the Christian life, it is important to be aware of the challenges and obstacles that can hinder our spiritual growth and effectiveness. Ephesians 6:12 reminds us, "For we wrestle not against flesh and blood, but against principalities, against powers, against the rulers of the darkness of this world, against spiritual wickedness in high places." Recognizing these challenges helps Christians prepare and rely on God's strength to overcome them.

In both NASCAR and the Christian life, teamwork is essential for executing a successful strategy. A driver relies on their pit crew, engineers, and spotters to provide support and guidance throughout the race. Similarly, Christians are part of the body of Christ and need the support and encouragement of fellow believers to stay on track. Hebrews

10:24-25 encourages us, "And let us consider one another to provoke unto love and to good works: Not forsaking the assembling of ourselves together, as the manner of some is; but exhorting one another: and so much the more, as ye see the day approaching." Being part of a supportive community helps Christians stay focused on their purpose and plan according to God's will.

Both NASCAR drivers and Christians must stay focused on their goals despite distractions and setbacks. During a race, a driver might face mechanical issues, accidents, or changes in weather that require quick thinking and adaptability. Similarly, Christians face various trials and temptations that can distract them from their purpose. James 1:2-4 encourages believers to remain steadfast, saying, "My brethren, count it all joy when ye fall into divers temptations; Knowing this, that the trying of your faith worketh patience. But let patience have her perfect work, that ye may be perfect and entire, wanting nothing." Staying focused on God's promises and relying on His strength helps Christians persevere through difficulties.

A well-executed race strategy in NASCAR involves regular evaluation and adjustment. Drivers and their teams continually assess their performance and make necessary changes to improve their chances of success. Similarly, Christians should regularly evaluate their spiritual lives and seek God's guidance for areas of growth and improvement. Psalm 139:23-24 says, "Search me, O God, and know my heart: try me, and know my thoughts: And see if there be any wicked way in me, and lead me in the way everlasting." Inviting God to examine our hearts and guide us helps ensure that we are living according to His will.

Trusting in God's plan also involves surrendering our own desires and understanding to Him. Just as a NASCAR driver trusts their crew chief's strategy, Christians must trust that God's plans are better than our own. Isaiah 55:8-9 says, "For my thoughts are not your thoughts, neither are your ways my ways, saith the LORD. For as the heavens are higher than the earth, so are my ways higher than your ways, and my thoughts than your thoughts." Surrendering to God's will and trusting His wisdom allows us to experience His best for our lives.

In NASCAR, a driver's preparation for the race is crucial to executing a successful strategy. This preparation includes physical training, studying the track, and understanding their car's capabilities. Similarly, Christians must prepare spiritually by spending time in prayer, studying the Bible, and seeking God's presence. Ephesians 6:10-11 encourages believers by stating "Finally, my brethren, be strong in the Lord, and in the power of his might. Put on the whole armour of God, that ye may be able to stand against the wiles of the devil." Spiritual preparation equips Christians to face life's challenges and stay aligned with God's plan.

Both NASCAR drivers and Christians benefit from the wisdom and experience of others. In racing, drivers often learn from more experienced teammates and coaches who provide valuable insights and advice. Similarly, Christians can learn from mentors and spiritual leaders who offer guidance and encouragement. Proverbs 15:22 says, "Without counsel purposes are disappointed: but in the multitude of counsellors they are established." Seeking the wisdom of others helps Christians grow in their faith and make wise decisions.

A successful race strategy in NASCAR also involves setting specific goals and milestones. Drivers and their teams set targets for each segment of the race, helping them stay focused and measure their progress. Similarly, Christians can set spiritual goals to help them grow in their faith and fulfill God's purposes. Philippians 3:13-14 says, "Brethren, I count not myself to have apprehended: but this one thing I do, forgetting those things which are behind, and reaching forth unto those things which are before, I press toward the mark for the prize of the high calling of God in Christ Jesus." Setting goals helps Christians stay focused on their spiritual journey and strive for growth and maturity.

In both NASCAR and the Christian life, resilience is key to staying on course and achieving success. During a race, a driver may face setbacks such as crashes or mechanical failures, but resilience allows them to keep going and adjust their strategy as needed. Similarly, Christians must be resilient in their faith, trusting God to help them overcome obstacles and remain faithful to His plan. Romans 8:28 encourages believers with the promise that " And we know that all things work together for good to them that love God, to them who are the called according to his purpose." Resilience and trust in God's goodness help Christians persevere through challenges and stay aligned with His will.

In NASCAR, a driver's mindset and attitude play a crucial role in executing their race strategy. Confidence, focus, and a positive attitude help drivers stay motivated and perform at their best. Similarly, Christians are called to have a mindset of faith and trust in God's promises. Philippians 4:8 encourages believers to focus on positive and virtuous things: "Finally, brethren, whatsoever things are true, whatsoever things are honest, whatsoever things are just, whatsoever things are pure, whatsoever things are lovely, whatsoever things are of good report; if there be any virtue, and if there be any praise, think on these things." Maintaining a positive and faith-filled attitude helps Christians stay focused on God's plan and navigate life's challenges with hope and confidence.

In both NASCAR and the Christian life, the ultimate goal is to finish well. For a NASCAR driver, finishing the race in a strong position, ideally winning, is the culmination of their efforts and strategy. Similarly, Christians strive to finish their spiritual race well, remaining faithful to God and fulfilling His purposes for their lives. 2 Timothy 4:7-8 expresses this goal: "I have fought a good fight, I have finished my course, I have kept the faith: Henceforth there is laid up for me a crown of righteousness, which the Lord, the righteous judge, shall give me at that day: and not to me only, but unto all them also that love his appearing." Finishing well means staying faithful to God's plan and trusting Him to lead us to the ultimate reward of eternal life with Him.

In conclusion, having a race strategy is essential for success in both NASCAR and the Christian life. NASCAR drivers plan their strategy to win the race, involving detailed preparation, teamwork, adaptability, and resilience. Similarly, Christians are called to live with a purpose and plan according to God's will. This involves seeking God's guidance, trusting His plan, being adaptable, and staying focused on the ultimate goal of glorifying Him and fulfilling His purposes. Proverbs 3:5-6 reminds us to "trust in the LORD with all thine heart; and lean not unto thine own understanding. In all thy ways acknowledge him, and he shall direct thy paths." By trusting God and following His guidance, Christians can navigate life's challenges, grow in their faith, and finish their spiritual race well, ultimately receiving the reward of eternal life with God.

24

Chapter 8 Perseverance

Perseverance is a vital quality in both NASCAR and the Christian life, as it enables individuals to push through difficult conditions and challenges to achieve their goals. In NASCAR, drivers must persevere through a variety of tough situations during races. They face high speeds, tight turns, changing weather conditions, and the constant threat of accidents or mechanical failures. Despite these challenges, drivers remain focused and determined, continually pushing themselves and their cars to the limit. The ability to persevere is what separates successful drivers from the rest, as they must maintain their concentration and composure under pressure, make quick decisions, and adapt to the everchanging circumstances on the track. Pit crews also play a crucial role in this process, providing support and making necessary adjustments to the car, ensuring that it remains in optimal condition for the race. The perseverance of both the driver and the team is essential for overcoming obstacles and achieving success in the highly competitive world of NASCAR.

Similarly, in the Christian life, believers are called to persevere through trials and tribulations. The Bible teaches that facing difficulties is a natural part of the Christian journey and that these challenges can help strengthen our faith and character. Romans 5:3-4 says, "And not only so, but we glory in tribulations also: knowing that tribulation worketh patience; And patience, experience; and experience, hope." This verse highlights the importance of perseverance, as enduring trials can lead to spiritual growth and a deeper sense of hope. Christians face various challenges, such as personal struggles, opposition, and temptations, which can test their faith and commitment to God. By persevering through these trials, believers can develop greater patience, gain valuable experience, and strengthen their hope in God's promises.

In NASCAR, perseverance involves physical endurance as well as mental toughness. Drivers must maintain their stamina throughout the race, often spending hours behind the wheel, enduring the physical strain of high-speed driving and the mental fatigue of constant focus. This requires rigorous training and preparation, as drivers work on their fitness and mental resilience to ensure they can handle the demands of the race. Similarly, Christians must develop spiritual endurance and mental toughness to persevere through life's challenges. This involves regular spiritual practices such as prayer, Bible study, and worship, which help strengthen our faith and keep us connected to God. By nurturing our relationship with God and relying on His strength, we can build the resilience needed to face trials and remain steadfast in our faith.

Both NASCAR drivers and Christians must also learn to adapt and remain flexible in the face of challenges. During a race, drivers may encounter unexpected obstacles such as crashes, mechanical issues, or changes in weather conditions. These situations require quick thinking and the ability to adjust their strategy on the fly. Perseverance means being able to stay calm and focused, making the necessary adjustments to continue moving forward. Similarly, Christians must be prepared to adapt to the unexpected challenges that life brings. This requires trusting in God's guidance as taught according to Isaiah 55:8-9 "For my thoughts are not your thoughts, neither are your ways my ways, saith the Lord. For as the heavens are higher than the earth, so are my ways higher than your ways, and my thoughts than your thoughts." By remaining flexible and open to God's leading, we can navigate life's trials with greater confidence and perseverance.

Another important aspect of perseverance in both NASCAR and the Christian life is the support and encouragement of others. In NASCAR, drivers rely on their pit crews, engineers, and spotters to provide the necessary support and guidance throughout the race. This teamwork and collaboration are essential for overcoming challenges and achieving success. Similarly, Christians benefit from the support and encouragement of fellow believers. Being part of a community of faith provides the strength and encouragement needed to persevere through difficult times. Hebrews 10:24-25 encourages believers to support one another: "And let us consider one another to provoke unto love and to good works: Not forsaking the assembling of ourselves together, as the manner of some is; but exhorting one another: and so much the more, as ye see the day approaching." By supporting and encouraging one another, believers can help each other stay strong in their faith and persevere through trials.

In both NASCAR and the Christian life, perseverance involves maintaining a positive attitude and outlook. Drivers must stay focused on their goals and remain optimistic, even when faced with setbacks or difficulties. A positive mindset helps them stay motivated and resilient, enabling them to push through challenges and continue striving for success. Similarly, Christians are called to maintain a positive attitude and trust in God's promises, even in the midst of trials. Philippians 4:8 encourages believers to focus on positive and virtuous things: "Finally, brethren, whatsoever things are true, whatsoever things are honest, whatsoever things are just, whatsoever things are pure, whatsoever things are lovely, whatsoever things are of good report; if there be any virtue, and if there be any praise, think on these things." By maintaining a focused view on God's goodness, Christians can find the strength to persevere through difficult times.

Perseverance also involves learning from experiences and using them to grow and improve. In NASCAR, drivers and their teams analyze each race, identifying areas for improvement and making necessary adjustments for future races. This process of reflection and learning helps them become better competitors and increases their chances of success. Similarly, Christians are encouraged to learn from their experiences and use them for spiritual growth. James 1:2-4 reminds believers that trials can lead to maturity and completeness: " My brethren, count it all joy when ye fall into divers temptations; Knowing this, that the trying of your faith worketh patience. But let patience have her perfect work, that ye may be perfect and entire, wanting nothing.." By reflecting on our experiences and seeking God's guidance, we can grow in our faith and become more resilient in the face of challenges.

Both NASCAR drivers and Christians must also cultivate patience as part of their perseverance. In a race, drivers must be patient, knowing when to push forward and when to hold back. Impatience can lead to mistakes, accidents, or poor decisions that can jeopardize their chances of success. Similarly, Christians are called to be patient in their faith journey, trusting in God's timing and plan. Patience is a key component of perseverance, as it helps believers remain steadfast and wait on God's perfect timing. Romans 12:12 encourages believers to be "Rejoicing in hope; patient in tribulation; continuing instant in prayer." By cultivating patience, Christians can better navigate trials and trust in God's plan for their lives.

In NASCAR, perseverance is often fueled by a strong sense of purpose and determination. Drivers are driven by their passion for the sport and their desire to win. This sense of purpose helps them stay motivated and committed, even when faced with obstacles. Similarly, Christians are called to live with a sense of purpose and determination, knowing that their ultimate goal is to glorify God and fulfill His purposes. Colossians 3:23-24 encourages believers to work with all their heart, as working for the Lord: "And whatsoever ye do, do it heartily, as to the Lord, and not unto men; Knowing that of the Lord ye shall receive the reward of the inheritance: for ye serve the Lord Christ." This sense of purpose helps Christians stay focused and persevere through trials, knowing that their efforts are for God's glory.

Perseverance in both NASCAR and the Christian life also involves resilience in the face of setbacks. In a race, drivers may encounter setbacks such as crashes, mechanical failures, or falling behind in the competition. Resilience allows them to recover from these setbacks, make necessary adjustments, and continue striving for success. Similarly, Christians may face setbacks in their faith journey, such as personal failures, disappointments, or opposition. Resilience helps believers bounce back from these setbacks, trust in God's grace, and continue pursuing their spiritual growth. Proverbs 24:16 reminds us that " For a just man falleth seven times, and riseth up again: but the wicked shall fall into mischief." By cultivating resilience, Christians can persevere through setbacks and remain steadfast in their faith.

Another important aspect of perseverance is the ability to stay focused on the ultimate goal. In NASCAR, drivers keep their eyes on the finish line, staying focused on their goal of winning the race. This focus helps them stay motivated and committed, even when the race becomes challenging. Similarly, Christians are called to keep their eyes on the ultimate goal of eternal life with God. Hebrews 12:1-2 encourages believers to run the race with perseverance, fixing their eyes on Jesus: "Wherefore seeing we also are compassed about with so great a cloud of witnesses, let us lay aside every weight, and the sin which doth so easily beset us, and let us run with patience the race that is set before us, Looking unto Jesus the author and finisher of our faith; who for the joy that was set before him endured the cross, despising the shame, and is set down at the right hand of the throne of God." By staying focused on Jesus and the promises of God, Christians can find the strength to persevere through life's challenges.

In both NASCAR and the Christian life, perseverance is often tested in the most difficult moments. During a race, drivers may face intense pressure, fatigue, and difficult conditions that test their endurance and determination. Similarly, Christians may face times of intense trial and suffering that test their faith and perseverance. James 1:12 offers encouragement to those who persevere: "Blessed is the man that endureth temptation: for when he is tried, he shall receive the crown of life, which the Lord hath promised to them that love him." This promise reminds believers that perseverance through trials is rewarded by God and leads to greater spiritual blessings.

Perseverance also involves trusting in the process and believing that the efforts and struggles will lead to a positive outcome. In NASCAR, drivers trust that their training, preparation, and the support of their team will help them succeed. They believe that their perseverance will pay off in the end. Similarly, Christians are called to trust in God's process and believe that their perseverance through trials will lead to spiritual growth and greater blessings. Romans 8:28 assures us that " And we know that all things work together for good to them that love God, to them who are the called according to his purpose." By trusting in God's plan and persevering through challenges, Christians can experience the fulfillment of His promises.

In conclusion, perseverance is a crucial quality in both NASCAR and the Christian life. NASCAR drivers must persevere through difficult conditions, maintaining their focus, determination, and resilience to achieve success. Similarly, Christians are called to persevere through trials, trusting in God's guidance and strength. Romans 5:3-4 reminds us that perseverance through tribulations leads to spiritual growth and hope: "And not only so, but we glory in tribulations also: knowing that tribulation worketh patience; And patience, experience; and experience, hope." By cultivating perseverance, Christians can navigate life's challenges, grow in their faith, and ultimately fulfill God's purposes for their lives. Just as NASCAR drivers rely on their training, preparation, and the support of their team, Christians rely on spiritual practices, the support of fellow believers, and their trust in God's promises to persevere through trials and remain steadfast in their faith. Through perseverance, both NASCAR drivers and Christians can achieve their ultimate goals and experience the rewards of their efforts.

Chapter 9 Race for the Prize

IN NASCAR, DRIVERS race for the trophy, and this quest for victory drives everything they do. From the moment a driver decides to pursue a career in racing, their life becomes a series of intense preparations, practice sessions, and strategic planning. The trophy represents not just a physical prize but also the culmination of countless hours of hard work, dedication, and sacrifice. Winning a race means being the best on that day, having the fastest car, making the smartest decisions, and sometimes just having the most luck. It's about being able to push through challenges, stay focused amidst high speeds and tight competition, and navigate the everchanging conditions on the track. Drivers must constantly improve their skills, learn from past races, and work closely with their teams to fine-tune their cars. The race for the prize in NASCAR is a grueling, high-stakes competition that demands the best from every driver and team member.

Similarly, in the Christian life, believers strive for the eternal prize. This prize is not a trophy or a medal but something far more valuable: eternal life with God. The Bible encourages Christians to run their spiritual race with the same intensity and determination as athletes competing for a prize. 1 Corinthians 9:24 says, "Know ye not that they which run in a race run all, but one receiveth the prize? So run, that ye may obtain." This verse emphasizes the importance of putting forth our best effort in our spiritual journey. Just as a driver gives everything they have on the track, Christians are called to live their lives with purpose and dedication, seeking to honor God in all they do.

The race for the prize in the Christian life involves several key components. First, it requires preparation. Just as NASCAR drivers spend countless hours practicing and preparing for races, Christians must also prepare for their spiritual journey. This preparation involves studying the Bible, spending time in prayer, and engaging in worship and fellowship with other believers. These practices help build a strong foundation of faith and equip Christians with the knowledge and strength they need to navigate life's challenges. Psalm 119:105 says, "Thy word is a lamp unto my feet, and a light unto my path," highlighting the importance of God's Word in guiding us on our journey.

Another essential aspect of racing for the prize is perseverance. NASCAR drivers face numerous obstacles on the track, from mechanical failures to fierce competition, and they must persevere through these challenges to reach the finish line. Similarly, Christians face trials and tribulations that test their faith and commitment. James 1:12 says, "Blessed is the man that endureth temptation: for when he is tried, he shall receive the crown of life, which the Lord hath promised to them that love him." Perseverance in the face of adversity strengthens our faith and brings us closer to God.

In NASCAR, strategy plays a crucial role in winning the race. Drivers and their teams develop detailed plans for when to make pit stops, how to conserve fuel and tires, and how to respond to different track conditions. This strategic thinking is essential for staying competitive and maximizing performance. Similarly, Christians must live with a purpose and plan according to God's will. Proverbs 3:5-6 advises, "Trust in the LORD with all thine heart; and lean not unto thine own understanding. In all thy ways acknowledge him, and he shall direct thy paths." Trusting in God's plan and seeking His guidance helps us make wise decisions and stay on the right path.

Teamwork is another critical component in the race for the prize. In NASCAR, the driver relies on the support and expertise of their pit crew, engineers, and spotters. This team effort ensures that the car is in top condition and that the driver has the information they need to make quick decisions. Similarly, Christians benefit from being part of a community of faith. Fellow believers provide encouragement, support, and accountability, helping us stay strong in our faith and overcome challenges. Hebrews 10:24-25 says, "And let us consider one another to provoke unto love and to good works: Not forsaking the assembling of ourselves together, as the manner of some is; but exhorting one another: and so much the more, as ye see the day approaching." Being part of a supportive Christian community helps us grow and persevere in our spiritual journey.

Focus and discipline are also essential in the race for the prize. NASCAR drivers must maintain intense focus throughout the race, avoiding distractions and staying committed to their strategy. This level of focus requires discipline and mental toughness. Similarly, Christians must stay focused on their spiritual goals, avoiding distractions that can lead them away from God. Hebrews 12:1-2 encourages believers by stating "Wherefore seeing we also are compassed about with so great a cloud of witnesses, let us lay aside every weight, and the sin which doth so easily beset us, and let us run with patience the race that is set before us, Looking unto Jesus the author and finisher of our faith; who for the joy that was set before him endured the cross, despising the shame, and is set down at the right hand of the throne of God." By keeping our eyes on Jesus and staying disciplined in our faith, we can run our spiritual race with perseverance.

In both NASCAR and the Christian life, resilience is key. During a race, drivers may encounter setbacks such as crashes or mechanical issues, but resilience allows them to recover and continue striving for victory. Similarly, Christians may face setbacks in their faith journey, such as personal failures, disappointments, or opposition. Resilience helps believers bounce back from these setbacks, trust in God's grace, and continue pursuing their spiritual growth. Proverbs 24:16 reminds us that "For a just man falleth seven times, and riseth up again: but the wicked shall fall into mischief." By cultivating resilience, Christians can persevere through setbacks and remain steadfast in their faith.

The ultimate goal in both NASCAR and the Christian life is to finish well. For a NASCAR driver, winning the race and receiving the trophy is the culmination of their efforts and dedication. Similarly, Christians strive to finish their spiritual race well, remaining faithful to God and fulfilling His purposes. 2 Timothy 4:7-8 expresses this goal: "I have fought a good fight, I have finished my course, I have kept the faith: Henceforth there is laid up for me a crown of righteousness, which the Lord, the righteous judge, shall give me at that day: and not to me only, but unto all them also that love his appearing." Finishing well means staying faithful to God's plan and trusting Him to lead us to the ultimate reward of eternal life with Him.

Both NASCAR drivers and Christians benefit from the wisdom and experience of others. In racing, drivers often learn from more experienced teammates and coaches who provide valuable insights and advice. Similarly, Christians can learn from mentors and spiritual leaders who offer guidance and encouragement. Proverbs 15:22 says, "Without counsel purposes are disappointed: but in the multitude of counsellors they are established." Seeking the wisdom of others helps Christians grow in their faith and make wise decisions.

Setting specific goals and milestones is another important aspect of racing for the prize. In NASCAR, drivers and their teams set targets for each segment of the race, helping them stay focused and measure their progress. Similarly, Christians can set spiritual goals to help them grow in their faith and fulfill God's purposes. Philippians 3:13-14 says, "Brethren, I count not myself to have apprehended: but this one thing I do, forgetting those things which are behind, and reaching forth unto those things which are before, I press toward the mark for the prize of the high calling of God in Christ Jesus." Setting goals helps Christians stay focused on their spiritual journey and strive for growth and maturity.

Resilience in the face of setbacks is another key aspect of racing for the prize. In a race, drivers may encounter setbacks such as crashes, mechanical failures, or falling behind in the competition. Resilience allows them to recover from these setbacks, make necessary adjustments, and continue striving for success. Similarly, Christians may face setbacks in their faith journey, such as personal failures, disappointments, or opposition. Resilience helps believers bounce back from these setbacks, trust in God's grace, and continue pursuing their spiritual growth. Proverbs 24:16 reminds us that "a just man falleth seven times, and riseth up again: but the wicked shall fall into mischief." By cultivating resilience, Christians can persevere through setbacks and remain steadfast in their faith.

The mindset and attitude of a driver are crucial in the race for the prize. Confidence, focus, and a positive attitude help drivers stay motivated and perform at their best. Similarly,

Christians are called to have a mindset of faith and trust in God's promises. Philippians 4:8 encourages believers to focus on Biblical things: "Finally, brethren, whatsoever things are true, whatsoever things are honest, whatsoever things are just, whatsoever things are pure, whatsoever things are lovely, whatsoever things are of good report; if there be any virtue, and if there be any praise, think on these things." Maintaining a faith-filled attitude helps Christians stay focused on God's plan and navigate life's challenges with hope and confidence.

In both NASCAR and the Christian life, the ultimate goal is to finish well. For a NASCAR driver, finishing the race in a strong position, ideally winning, is the culmination of their efforts and strategy. Similarly, Christians strive to finish their spiritual race well, remaining faithful to God and fulfilling His purposes for their lives. 2 Timothy 4:7-8 expresses this goal: "I have fought a good fight, I have finished my course, I have kept the faith: Henceforth there is laid up for me a crown of righteousness, which the Lord, the righteous judge, shall give me at that day: and not to me only, but unto all them also that love his appearing." Finishing well means staying faithful to God's plan and trusting Him to lead us to the ultimate reward of eternal life with Him.

In conclusion, racing for the prize is essential in both NASCAR and the Christian life. NASCAR drivers race for the trophy, involving detailed preparation, teamwork, adaptability, and resilience. Similarly, Christians strive for the eternal prize, involving seeking God's guidance, trusting His plan, being adaptable, and staying focused on the ultimate goal of glorifying Him and fulfilling His purposes. 1 Corinthians 9:24 reminds us to run our spiritual race with determination and purpose: "Know ye not that they which run in a race run all, but one receiveth the prize? So run, that ye may obtain.." By trusting God and following His guidance, Christians can navigate life's challenges, grow in their faith, and finish their spiritual race well, ultimately receiving the reward of eternal life with God.

Chapter 10 Training

TRAINING IS CRUCIAL for both NASCAR drivers and Christians as it helps them to grow, improve, and achieve their goals. In NASCAR, drivers train and practice regularly to hone their skills and prepare for the intense demands of racing. This training involves physical exercise to build strength and stamina, mental exercises to improve focus and decision making, and hours of practice on the track to perfect their driving techniques. Drivers need to be in peak physical condition to withstand the physical strain of high-speed racing and the intense G-forces they experience during sharp turns and sudden accelerations. They also work on their reflexes and hand-eye coordination, as split-second decisions can make the difference between winning and losing a race. Additionally, drivers study race tracks, learn about their cars' mechanics, and analyze past performances to identify areas for improvement. This comprehensive training regimen ensures that they are well-prepared for the challenges they will face on race day.

Similarly, Christians grow through spiritual disciplines, which are practices that help them develop a deeper relationship with God and grow in godliness. Just as a NASCAR driver needs to train regularly to improve their performance, Christians need to engage in spiritual disciplines consistently to grow in their faith. These disciplines include prayer, reading and studying the Bible, worship, fellowship with other believers, fasting, and serving others. Prayer is a vital spiritual discipline that allows Christians to communicate with God, seek His guidance, and draw strength from His presence. It is through prayer that believers can express their gratitude, confess their sins, and intercede for others. Reading and studying the Bible is another essential discipline, as it helps Christians understand God's will, learn His promises, and apply His teachings to their lives. The Bible serves as a guide and a source of wisdom, providing direction and encouragement for the Christian journey.

Worship is another important discipline, as it allows Christians to honor and glorify God. Worship can take many forms, including singing, praying, and giving thanks. It is a way for believers to express their love and reverence for God and to acknowledge His greatness and sovereignty. Fellowship with other believers is also crucial for spiritual growth. By gathering with other Christians, believers can encourage one another, share their experiences, and build strong, supportive relationships. This sense of community helps Christians stay accountable and motivated in their walk with God.

Fasting is a discipline that involves abstaining from food or other activities for a period of time to focus on prayer and seeking God's will. It is a way to humble oneself before God and to seek His guidance and strength. Serving others is another important discipline, as it reflects the love and compassion of Christ. By helping those in need, Christians can demonstrate their faith in action and make a positive impact in their communities.

1 Timothy 4:8 highlights the value of spiritual training: "For bodily exercise profiteth little: but godliness is profitable unto all things, having promise of the life that now is, and of that which is to come." This verse emphasizes that while physical exercise has some value, training in godliness has far greater benefits, both in this life and in the life to come. Just as physical training helps a NASCAR driver perform better on the track, spiritual training helps Christians live a more fulfilling and purposeful life, aligning their actions with God's will and growing in their relationship with Him.

Both NASCAR drivers and Christians must be disciplined and committed to their training. A driver who neglects their training will not perform well in races, and a Christian who neglects spiritual disciplines will struggle to grow in their faith. Consistency is key, as regular practice and engagement in these disciplines lead to steady growth and improvement. Just as a driver follows a training schedule, Christians can benefit from establishing a routine that includes time for prayer, Bible study, worship, and fellowship.

Training also involves setting goals and measuring progress. NASCAR drivers set specific goals for their performance, such as improving their lap times, mastering certain tracks, or achieving a higher fitness level. They track their progress and make adjustments to their training regimen as needed. Similarly, Christians can set spiritual goals, such as reading through the entire Bible in a year, spending a certain amount of time in prayer each day, or participating in a ministry or service project. By setting goals and tracking progress, believers can stay focused and motivated in their spiritual journey.

Both NASCAR drivers and Christians benefit from the guidance and support of others. Drivers often work with coaches, trainers, and mentors who provide valuable feedback, encouragement, and advice. These relationships help drivers stay accountable and motivated in their training. Similarly, Christians can seek guidance and support from spiritual mentors, pastors, and fellow believers. These relationships provide encouragement, accountability, and wisdom, helping believers grow in their faith and stay committed to their spiritual disciplines.

Training also requires perseverance and resilience. NASCAR drivers face numerous challenges in their training, such as physical fatigue, mental stress, and setbacks on the track. Perseverance is essential for pushing through these challenges and continuing to improve. Similarly, Christians face challenges in their spiritual journey, such as doubts, temptations, and trials. Perseverance is crucial for staying faithful to God and continuing to grow in godliness. James 1:12 says, "Blessed is the man that endureth temptation: for when he is tried, he shall receive the crown of life, which the Lord hath promised to them that love him." By persevering through challenges and remaining committed to their spiritual disciplines, Christians can grow stronger in their faith and receive the blessings that God has promised.

Both NASCAR drivers and Christians must also be adaptable and willing to adjust their training as needed. Drivers may need to modify their training regimen based on their performance, feedback from their coaches, or changes in their physical condition. Similarly, Christians may need to adjust their spiritual disciplines based on their current season of life, personal growth, and the leading of the Holy Spirit. Being flexible and open to change allows believers to continue growing and developing in their faith.

The ultimate goal of training for a NASCAR driver is to perform well in races and achieve success on the track.

Similarly, the ultimate goal of spiritual training for Christians is to grow in godliness and fulfill God's purposes for their lives. This involves becoming more like Christ, developing a deeper relationship with God, and living out one's faith in practical ways. Philippians 3:13-14 says, "Brethren, I count not myself to have apprehended: but this one thing I do, forgetting those things which are behind, and reaching forth unto those things which are before, I press toward the mark for the prize of the high calling of God in Christ Jesus." By staying focused on their spiritual goals and persevering in their training, Christians can grow in their faith and experience the fullness of life that God has for them.

In conclusion, training is essential for both NASCAR drivers and Christians, as it helps them to grow, improve, and achieve their goals. NASCAR drivers train and practice regularly to hone their skills and prepare for the demands of racing, while Christians grow through spiritual disciplines that help them develop a deeper relationship with God and grow in godliness. 1 Timothy 4:8 emphasizes the importance of spiritual training, highlighting that it has far greater benefits than physical exercise. Both NASCAR drivers and Christians must be disciplined and committed to their training, setting goals, measuring progress, and seeking guidance and support from others. Perseverance and resilience are crucial for pushing through challenges and continuing to grow, and adaptability allows for adjustments as needed. The ultimate goal of training for a NASCAR driver is to achieve success on the track, while the ultimate goal of spiritual training for Christians is to grow in godliness and fulfill God's purposes for their lives. By staying focused on their goals and remaining committed to their training, both NASCAR drivers and Christians can experience the rewards of their efforts and achieve their desired outcomes.

34

Chapter 11 Safety Gear

IN NASCAR, DRIVERS wear safety gear for protection, which is essential for their survival and performance on the track. This gear includes helmets, fireproof suits, gloves, shoes, and head and neck support devices (HANS). Each piece of equipment is designed to protect the driver from various dangers they might encounter during a race, such as highspeed collisions, fires, and debris. Helmets are crucial as they protect the head from impact injuries, while fireproof suits, gloves, and shoes protect the body from burns in case of a fire. The HANS device is designed to prevent head and neck injuries by limiting the movement of the head during a crash. This comprehensive safety gear is mandated by racing authorities to ensure that drivers are as safe as possible while competing in such a high-risk sport. The importance of this gear cannot be overstated, as it has saved countless lives and prevented numerous injuries over the years. Drivers trust their gear to keep them safe, allowing them to focus on their performance and race with confidence.

Similarly, in the Christian life, believers are called to put on the armor of God for spiritual protection. Just as NASCAR drivers need physical protection, Christians need spiritual protection to stand against the challenges and temptations they face in their daily lives. Ephesians 6:11 says, "Put on the whole armour of God, that ye may be able to stand against the wiles of the devil." This verse emphasizes the importance of being spiritually prepared and protected to withstand the schemes and attacks of the devil. The armor of God includes several key components, each with a specific purpose, much like the safety gear worn by NASCAR drivers.

The first piece of the armor of God is the belt of truth. In ancient times, a belt was used to hold a soldier's armor together and provide support. Similarly, the belt of truth represents the importance of living a life grounded in truth and integrity. For Christians, this means being honest, trustworthy, and standing firm in the truth of God's Word. Truth provides the foundation for a strong and secure spiritual life, much like a belt provides support for a soldier's armor.

The second piece is the breastplate of righteousness. The breastplate protects the vital organs, especially the heart, from attacks. In the same way, righteousness protects a Christian's heart and soul. Righteousness involves living a life that is pleasing to God, following His commandments, and striving to do what is right. It is a protective barrier against the temptations and corruptions of the world, helping believers maintain a pure and holy life.

The third piece is the footwear of the gospel of peace. Just as a soldier needs sturdy shoes to stand firm and move quickly in battle, Christians need the gospel of peace to stand firm in their faith and be ready to share the good news of Jesus Christ. The gospel provides a solid foundation for believers, giving them peace and confidence in their relationship with God. It also prepares them to go out and spread the message of salvation to others, bringing peace and hope to those who hear it.

The fourth piece is the shield of faith. A shield is used to deflect attacks and protect a soldier from harm. Similarly, faith acts as a shield for Christians, protecting them from the doubts, fears, and attacks of the enemy. Faith involves trusting in God's promises, believing in His power, and relying on His strength. It helps believers stand firm in the face of adversity, knowing that God is with them and will protect them.

The fifth piece is the helmet of salvation. A helmet protects the head, which is essential for survival in battle. In the same way, salvation protects a Christian's mind and assures them of their eternal life with God. The knowledge of salvation gives believers confidence and hope, helping them stay focused on their spiritual journey and resist the attacks of the enemy.

The sixth piece is the sword of the Spirit, which is the Word of God. A sword is a weapon used for offense and defense. Similarly, the Word of God is a powerful tool for Christians, helping them defend against the lies and temptations of the devil and stand firm in the truth. By studying and applying the Bible, believers can grow in their faith, gain wisdom, and effectively share the gospel with others.

In NASCAR, drivers not only wear their safety gear but also regularly inspect and maintain it to ensure it is in good condition. Similarly, Christians must regularly engage in spiritual practices such as prayer, Bible study, worship, and fellowship to keep their spiritual armor strong and effective. These practices help believers stay connected to God, grow in their faith, and remain vigilant against spiritual attacks.

Both NASCAR drivers and Christians must also trust in their protection. Drivers trust that their safety gear will protect them in the event of a crash, allowing them to focus on racing with confidence. Similarly, Christians must trust in the armor of God and believe that He will protect them from spiritual harm. This trust is built through a strong relationship with God, nurtured by regular prayer, worship, and studying His Word.

The importance of preparation cannot be overstated for both NASCAR drivers and Christians. Just as drivers prepare for races by ensuring their safety gear is ready, Christians must prepare for spiritual battles by putting on the full armor of God. This preparation involves being aware of potential dangers, understanding how to use their spiritual tools, and staying vigilant in their faith.

The analogy of the armor of God serves as a powerful reminder of the spiritual battles Christians face and the protection God provides. By putting on the armor of God, believers can stand firm against the schemes of the devil, resist temptation, and live a victorious Christian life. This spiritual armor equips them to face life's challenges with courage, confidence, and faith, knowing that God is with them and will help them overcome.

In conclusion, the concept of safety gear in NASCAR and the armor of God in the Christian life highlights the importance of protection, preparation, and trust. NASCAR drivers wear safety gear to protect themselves from physical harm, allowing them to focus on racing with confidence. Similarly, Christians are called to put on the armor of God for spiritual protection, enabling them to stand firm against the challenges and temptations they face. Ephesians 6:11 emphasizes the importance of this spiritual armor: "Put on the whole armour of God, that ye may be able to stand against the wiles of the devil." By regularly engaging in spiritual practices, trusting in God's protection, and being prepared for spiritual battles, Christians can live a victorious and fulfilling life, confident in the knowledge that God is with them and will protect them from harm.

Chapter 12 Supporters

IN NASCAR, FANS PLAY a crucial role in supporting drivers, creating an energetic and motivating atmosphere that can make a significant difference in a driver's performance. The relationship between drivers and their fans is a powerful one, as fans' cheers and encouragement boost drivers' morale and inspire them to push harder and achieve more. Fans show their support in many ways, such as attending races, wearing team merchandise, and cheering from the stands or from home. They celebrate victories and stand by their favorite drivers during tough times, providing a sense of community and belonging. This unwavering support helps drivers stay motivated, knowing they have a loyal fan base cheering them on every step of the way. Drivers often acknowledge the impact of their fans, expressing gratitude for their encouragement and recognizing that their success is, in part, due to the support they receive.

Similarly, in the Christian life, believers are called to encourage and support each other, creating a strong and uplifting community that helps individuals grow in their faith and navigate life's challenges. The Bible emphasizes the importance of mutual support and encouragement among Christians, as seen in 1 Thessalonians 5:11, which says, "Wherefore comfort yourselves together, and edify one another, even as also ye do." This verse highlights the need for Christians to encourage, providing comfort and support in times of need and celebrating each other's successes. Just as NASCAR drivers rely on the support of their fans, Christians rely on the leading of the Holy Ghost and the support of their fellow believers to stay strong in their faith and fulfill God's purposes.

In the Christian community, support comes in many forms. It can be as simple as a kind word, a prayer, or a helping hand during difficult times. Christians are encouraged to bear one another's burdens, as stated in Galatians 6:2: "Bear ye one another's burdens, and so fulfil the law of Christ." This means being there for each other in times of trouble, offering emotional, spiritual, and practical support. When believers support each other, they reflect the love of Christ and create a sense of unity and belonging within the community.

Encouragement is also a vital aspect of the Christian life. Just as fans cheer for their favorite NASCAR drivers, Christians are called to encourage one another in their faith. Hebrews 10:24-25 says, "And let us consider one another to provoke unto love and to good works: Not forsaking the assembling of ourselves together, as the manner of some is; but exhorting one another: and so much the more, as ye see the day approaching." This passage emphasizes the importance of meeting together regularly to encourage and motivate each other to live out their faith through love and good works. By gathering together for worship, Bible study, and fellowship, believers can strengthen their relationships with God and with each other, providing the encouragement needed to persevere in their spiritual journey.

Support and encouragement within the Christian community also involve recognizing and celebrating each other's achievements and spiritual growth. Just as NASCAR fans celebrate their favorite driver's victories, Christians should celebrate the milestones and accomplishments of their fellow believers. This can include recognizing personal growth, successful ministry efforts, and other significant achievements in one's faith journey. Romans 12:15 encourages believers to "Rejoice with them that do rejoice, and weep with them that weep," highlighting the importance of sharing in each other's joys and sorrows.

Mentorship is another important aspect of support in the Christian life. More experienced believers can provide guidance, wisdom, and encouragement to those who are newer in their faith. This mentorship helps individuals grow spiritually, navigate challenges, and develop a deeper understanding of God's Word. Proverbs 27:17 says, "Iron sharpeneth iron; so a man sharpeneth the countenance of his friend." By building strong, supportive relationships, believers can help each other become more effective and faithful followers of Christ.

Prayer is a powerful way for Christians to support one another. Praying for each other's needs, struggles, and spiritual growth helps to strengthen the bond between believers and invites God's presence and intervention in their lives. James 5:16 says, "Confess your faults one to another, and pray one for another, that ye may be healed. The effectual fervent prayer of a righteous man availeth much." By praying for each other, Christians can provide spiritual support and encouragement, helping to lift each other up and draw closer to God.

Support within the Christian community also involves offering practical help and assistance. Just as NASCAR fans might support their favorite driver by purchasing merchandise or attending races, Christians can support each other through acts of service. This can include providing meals for a family in need, helping with childcare, offering transportation, or assisting with household chores. Acts of service demonstrate the love and compassion of Christ and help to build a strong and caring community.

In times of crisis or difficulty, the support of fellow believers can be especially important. Just as fans rally around a driver who has experienced a setback or a crash, Christians are called to provide comfort and encouragement to those who are facing trials. 2 Corinthians 1:3-4 says, "Blessed be God, even the Father of our Lord Jesus Christ, the Father of mercies, and the God of all comfort; Who comforteth us in all our tribulation, that we may be able to comfort them which are in any trouble, by the comfort wherewith we ourselves are comforted of God." By offering comfort and support, believers can help each other find strength and hope in God's promises.

Support within the Christian community also involves accountability. Just as fans might hold a driver accountable for their actions on and off the track, Christians are called to hold each other accountable in their walk with God. This means lovingly confronting each other when necessary, encouraging repentance and growth, and helping each other stay true to their faith. Galatians 6:1 says, "Brethren, if a man be overtaken in a fault, ye which are spiritual, restore such an one in the spirit of meekness; considering thyself, lest thou also be tempted." Accountability helps believers stay on the right path and grow in their relationship with God.

Encouraging and supporting each other in the Christian life also involves building a strong sense of community. Just as

NASCAR fans create a sense of camaraderie and unity by coming together to support their favorite drivers, Christians are called to create a loving and supportive community where everyone feels valued and included. Acts 2:42-47 describes the early Christian community: "And they continued stedfastly in the apostles' doctrine and fellowship, and in breaking of bread, and in prayers. And fear came upon every soul: and many wonders and signs were done by the apostles. And all that believed were together, and had all things common; And sold their possessions and goods, and parted them to all men, as every man had need. And they, continuing daily with one accord in the temple, and breaking bread from house to house, did eat their meat with gladness and singleness of heart, Praising God, and having favour with all the people. And the Lord added to the church daily such as should be saved." This sense of mutual support within the local church helps believers grow in their faith and strengthens the body of Christ.

In conclusion, supporters play a crucial role in both NASCAR and the Christian life. NASCAR drivers rely on the support and encouragement of their fans to stay motivated and perform at their best. Similarly, Christians are called to encourage and support each other, creating a strong local church that helps individuals grow in their faith and navigate life's challenges. 1 Thessalonians 5:11 emphasizes the importance of mutual support and encouragement: "Wherefore comfort yourselves together, and edify one another, even as also ye do." By providing comfort, encouragement, prayer, practical help, mentorship, accountability within the local church, believers can build each other up and strengthen their relationship with God. Just as fans help drivers achieve success on the track, Christians help each other grow and fulfill God's purposes in their lives. Through mutual support and encouragement, the local church can reflect the love of Christ and create a welcoming and nurturing environment for all believers.

Chapter 13 Resilience

RESILIENCE IS A VITAL trait in both NASCAR and the Christian life, as it involves the ability to bounce back from crashes and recover from setbacks and failures. In NASCAR, drivers must demonstrate incredible resilience to navigate the highspeed, high-stakes world of racing. Crashes, mechanical failures, and other unexpected challenges are part of the sport, and drivers must be prepared to face these obstacles head-on. When a driver crashes, it can be a frightening and disheartening experience, but the most successful drivers are those who can quickly recover, assess the damage, and get back on the track. This resilience is not just about physical toughness but also about mental strength and determination. Drivers need to shake off the fear and frustration that come with crashes and focus on the task at hand. They rely on their pit crews and support teams to make quick repairs and adjustments, allowing them to continue racing. The ability to bounce back from these setbacks is what separates the good drivers from the great ones. It requires a combination of skill, confidence, and an unwavering belief in their abilities and the capabilities of their team.

Similarly, in the Christian life, believers are called to demonstrate resilience in the face of setbacks and failures. The journey of faith is filled with challenges, temptations, and moments of weakness, but Christians are encouraged to rise up and continue moving forward. Proverbs 24:16 says, "For a just man falleth seven times, and riseth up again: but the wicked shall fall into mischief." This verse highlights the importance of resilience, emphasizing that even righteous individuals will face falls and failures, but their strength lies in their ability to rise again. Christians are not promised a life free from difficulties, but they are given the assurance that God's grace and strength will help them overcome these obstacles.

In both NASCAR and the Christian life, resilience involves learning from setbacks and using those experiences to grow stronger. When a NASCAR driver crashes, they and their team analyze what went wrong, make necessary adjustments, and apply those lessons to future races. This process of reflection and improvement is crucial for long-term success. Similarly, Christians are encouraged to reflect on their setbacks, seek God's guidance, and learn from their experiences. Romans 5:3-4 says, "And not only so, but we glory in tribulations also: knowing that tribulation worketh patience; And patience, experience; and experience, hope." Through trials and tribulations, believers develop patience and gain valuable experience, which ultimately strengthens their hope and faith.

Resilience also involves relying on a support system. In NASCAR, drivers depend on their pit crews, engineers, and team members to help them recover from crashes and continue racing. This teamwork and support are essential for overcoming challenges and achieving success. Similarly, Christians rely on their spiritual community for support and encouragement. Fellow believers provide prayer, guidance, and a listening ear, helping individuals navigate their setbacks and stay strong in their faith. Galatians 6:2 says, "Bear ye one another's burdens, and so fulfil the law of Christ." By supporting each other, Christians can build resilience and continue their spiritual journey with confidence.

Another important aspect of resilience is maintaining a positive attitude and perspective. NASCAR drivers who remain optimistic and focused on their goals are more likely to recover quickly from setbacks and perform well in future races. This positive mindset helps them stay motivated and resilient in the face of adversity. Similarly, Christians are called to maintain a Christlike attitude and trust in God's promises, even during difficult times. Philippians 4:13 reminds believers, "I can do all things through Christ which strengtheneth me." By focusing on God's strength and promises, Christians can find the resilience needed to overcome setbacks and continue growing in their faith.

Resilience also involves perseverance and determination. In NASCAR, drivers must persevere through long races, physical fatigue, and the mental strain of high-speed competition. This determination helps them push through challenging moments and stay focused on their goals.

Similarly, Christians are called to persevere in their faith, even when faced with trials and temptations. James 1:12 says, "Blessed is the man that endureth temptation: for when he is tried, he shall receive the crown of life, which the Lord hath promised to them that love him." Perseverance in the face of adversity is a key component of resilience and leads to spiritual growth and rewards.

Both NASCAR drivers and Christians must also develop flexibility and adaptability. On the racetrack, conditions can change rapidly, and drivers need to adapt their strategies to respond to these changes. This flexibility helps them navigate unexpected challenges and continue competing effectively. Similarly, Christians must be adaptable in their spiritual journey, ready to adjust their plans and approaches as they seek God's guidance. Proverbs 3:5-6 encourages believers to trust in God's direction: "Trust in the LORD with all thine heart; and lean not unto thine own understanding. In all thy ways acknowledge him, and he shall direct thy paths." By being flexible and open to God's leading, Christians can build resilience and navigate life's challenges more effectively.

In NASCAR, drivers often face multiple setbacks within a single race, requiring them to demonstrate resilience repeatedly. They may experience tire blowouts, engine failures, or collisions, but the ability to bounce back and keep racing is crucial. Similarly, Christians may face multiple challenges and setbacks in their faith journey, but resilience involves continually rising up and moving forward. 2 Corinthians 4:8-9 says, "We are troubled on every side, yet not distressed; we are perplexed, but not in despair; Persecuted, but not forsaken; cast down, but not destroyed." This resilience is rooted in the knowledge that God is with them, providing strength and support through every trial.

Resilience also involves accepting and learning from failures. In NASCAR, drivers understand that crashes and mistakes are part of the sport. They learn to accept these failures, analyze what went wrong, and use that knowledge to improve. Similarly, Christians must learn to accept their failures and imperfections, seeking God's forgiveness and grace. 1 John 1:9 assures believers, "If we confess our sins, he is faithful and just to forgive us our sins, and to cleanse us from all unrighteousness." By acknowledging their mistakes and seeking God's grace, Christians can build resilience and continue growing in their faith.

Another important aspect of resilience is the ability to keep sight of the bigger picture. In NASCAR, drivers are focused on the ultimate goal of winning the race or the championship, which helps them stay motivated and resilient in the face of setbacks. Similarly, Christians are called to keep their eyes on the eternal prize, the hope of eternal life with God. This focus helps them stay resilient and motivated, even when facing trials and difficulties. Philippians 3:13-14 says, "Brethren, I count not myself to have apprehended: but this one thing I do, forgetting those things which are behind, and reaching forth unto those things which are before, I press toward the mark for the prize of the high calling of God in Christ Jesus." By keeping their focus on God's promises and the hope of eternal life, Christians can find the strength to persevere through setbacks.

Resilience in both NASCAR and the Christian life also involves self-discipline and commitment. Drivers must be disciplined in their training, preparation, and race strategies to stay competitive and recover from setbacks. Similarly,

Christians must be disciplined in their spiritual practices, such as prayer, Bible study, and worship, to build resilience and stay strong in their faith. 1 Corinthians 9:25 says, "And every man that striveth for the mastery is temperate in all things. Now they do it to obtain a corruptible crown; but we an incorruptible." This discipline helps believers stay focused on their spiritual goals and build the resilience needed to overcome challenges.

In conclusion, resilience is a crucial trait in both NASCAR and the Christian life, as it involves the ability to bounce back from crashes and recover from setbacks and failures. NASCAR drivers demonstrate resilience through their physical toughness, mental strength, and determination, relying on their support teams and learning from their experiences to continue competing. Similarly, Christians are called to demonstrate resilience in their faith journey, rising up after setbacks, learning from their experiences, and relying on God's strength and support. Proverbs 24:16 emphasizes the importance of resilience: "For a just man falleth seven times, and riseth up again: but the wicked shall fall into mischief." By maintaining a Christlike attitude, trusting in God's promises, and supporting one another, Christians can build resilience and continue growing in their faith.

Chapter 14 Unity

UNITY IS ESSENTIAL in both NASCAR and the Christian life, as it allows teams and the church to work together seamlessly toward their goals. In NASCAR, the success of a driver is not just dependent on their skill behind the wheel but also on the collective effort of their entire team. This includes the pit crew, engineers, mechanics, and strategists who work together to ensure the car is in peak condition and that the driver has the best possible chance of winning. The pit crew must perform lightning-fast tire changes, refuel the car, and make necessary adjustments during pit stops, all in a matter of seconds. Engineers and mechanics work tirelessly behind the scenes to fine-tune the car, ensuring it can handle the rigors of high-speed racing. Strategists analyze data and track conditions to develop race strategies that give the driver a competitive edge. Communication and coordination are crucial, as even the smallest mistake can cost valuable time and potentially the race. This level of unity requires trust, respect, and a shared commitment to the team's goals. When everyone works together seamlessly, the team can overcome challenges and achieve success on the track.

Similarly, in the Christian life, the church is called to work together in unity to fulfill God's purposes. The Bible emphasizes the importance of unity among believers, as seen in Psalm 133:1, which says, "Behold, how good and how pleasant it is for brethren to dwell together in unity!" This verse highlights the beauty and strength that come from believers living and working together in harmony. The church is made up of many members, each with unique gifts and roles, but all are essential to the functioning of the body of Christ. Just as a NASCAR team relies on the diverse skills of its members, the church relies on the diverse gifts of its members to carry out its mission.

In the church, unity means working together to support one another, share the gospel, and magnify the Lord. This involves regular fellowship, worship, prayer, and Bible study, which help to strengthen relationships and point people to Christ. Ephesians 4:3 encourages believers to "endeavor to keep the unity of the Spirit in the bond of peace." This unity is not just about getting along but about working together with a shared purpose and vision. It requires humility, patience, and a willingness to put others' needs before our own. When the church operates in unity, it reflects the love of Christ to the world and becomes a powerful force for God that impacts eternity.

In both NASCAR and the church, communication is key to maintaining unity. NASCAR teams use headsets and other communication tools to stay in constant contact during a race, ensuring everyone is on the same page and can respond quickly to changing conditions. Similarly, in the church, open and honest communication helps to build trust, resolve conflicts, and ensure that everyone is working toward the same goals. Ephesians 4:15-16 encourages believers to "But speaking the truth in love, may grow up into him in all things, which is the head, even Christ: From whom the whole body fitly joined together and compacted by that which every joint supplieth, according to the effectual working in the measure of every part, maketh increase of the body unto the edifying of itself in love." This passage emphasizes the importance of communication and cooperation in building a strong and unified church.

Another important aspect of unity is mutual support and encouragement. In NASCAR, team members support each other by sharing knowledge, providing feedback, and helping one another improve. This mutual support helps to build a strong team dynamic and fosters a sense of camaraderie. Similarly, in the church, believers are called to support and encourage one another. Hebrews 10:24-25 says, "And let us consider one another to provoke unto love and to good works: Not forsaking the assembling of ourselves together, as the manner of some is; but exhorting one another: and so much the more, as ye see the day approaching." By supporting and encouraging each other, believers can build a strong and unified church community.

Unity also involves working together to achieve common goals. In NASCAR, the team's goal is to win races and championships, and everyone works together to achieve this. Each member of the team has a specific role, and their combined efforts contribute to the overall success of the team. Similarly, the church has a common goal of spreading the gospel and making disciples of all nations. This involves evangelism, discipleship, and service, all of which require the collective effort of the entire church body. 1 Corinthians 12:12-14 says, "For as the body is one, and hath many members, and all the members of that one body, being many, are one body: so also is Christ. For by one Spirit are we all baptized into one body, whether we be Jews or Gentiles, whether we be bond or free; and have been all made to drink into one Spirit. For the body is not one member, but many." This passage highlights the importance of each member's contribution to the overall mission of the church.

In both NASCAR and the church, unity requires a shared vision and commitment to the team's goals. NASCAR teams have a clear vision of what they want to achieve and work together to make it happen. This involves setting goals, developing strategies, and staying focused on the task at hand. Similarly, the church must have a clear vision and mission, and every member must be committed to working toward that vision. Proverbs 29:18 says, "Where there is no vision, the people perish: but he that keepeth the law, happy is he." A shared vision helps to unify the church and keep everyone focused on the same goals.

Unity also involves celebrating successes and learning from failures. In NASCAR, teams celebrate victories together, recognizing the contributions of each member. They also analyze their performance after each race, identifying areas for improvement and making necessary adjustments.

Similarly, in the church, believers are called to rejoice with those who rejoice and to weep with those who weep (Romans 12:15). Celebrating successes and supporting each other through challenges helps to build a strong and unified church family. It also involves learning from mistakes and seeking God's guidance for growth and improvement.

In both NASCAR and the church, unity is strengthened through shared experiences and teamwork. NASCAR teams spend countless hours practicing, strategizing, and racing together, which builds strong bonds and a sense of camaraderie. Similarly, the church strengthens its unity through shared experiences such as worship, prayer, service projects, and fellowship events. These shared experiences help to build relationships, foster trust, and create a sense of belonging. Acts 2:42-47 describes the early church's commitment to unity and fellowship: "And they continued stedfastly in the apostles' doctrine and fellowship, and in breaking of bread, and in prayers. And fear came upon every soul: and many wonders and signs were done by the apostles. And all that believed were together, and had all things common; And sold their possessions and goods, and parted them to all men, as every man had need. And they, continuing daily with one accord in the temple, and breaking bread from house to house, did eat their meat with gladness and singleness of heart, Praising God, and having favour with all the people. And the Lord added to the church daily such as should be saved." This passage highlights the importance of shared experiences and teamwork in building a strong and unified church.

In conclusion, unity is essential in both NASCAR and the Christian life, as it allows teams and the church to work together seamlessly toward their goals. NASCAR teams rely on the collective effort of their members, including the pit crew, engineers, mechanics, and strategists, to ensure the car is in peak condition and that the driver has the best possible chance of winning. Similarly, the church relies on the diverse gifts and contributions of its members to fulfill God's purposes and spread the gospel. Psalm 133:1 emphasizes the beauty and strength of unity: "Behold, how good and how pleasant it is for brethren to dwell together in unity!" By maintaining open communication, providing mutual support and encouragement, working toward common goals, celebrating successes, learning from failures, and sharing experiences, both NASCAR teams and the church can build strong, unified communities that achieve great things to the honor and glory of God.

46

Chapter 15 Determination

DETERMINATION IS CRUCIAL in both NASCAR and the Christian life, as it drives individuals to pursue their goals with relentless effort and unwavering focus. In NASCAR, drivers are determined to win, putting in countless hours of training, practice, and preparation to improve their skills and enhance their performance on the track. This determination is evident in their dedication to physical fitness, mental toughness, and strategic planning. NASCAR drivers face intense competition and numerous challenges, such as high speeds, tight turns, and the constant risk of crashes. Despite these obstacles, their determination keeps them focused on the goal of crossing the finish line first. They push through fatigue, overcome setbacks, and continuously strive to be better. This determination is not just about individual effort but also about the collective determination of the entire team, including the pit crew, engineers, and strategists, who work together to ensure the car performs optimally and the driver has the best possible chance of winning.

Similarly, in the Christian life, believers are called to be determined in their pursuit of following Christ. This determination involves a steadfast commitment to living according to God's will, growing in faith, and spreading the message of the gospel. Philippians 3:14 encapsulates this determination: "I press toward the mark for the prize of the high calling of God in Christ Jesus." This verse emphasizes the importance of pressing forward with purpose and resolve, striving to fulfill the calling that God has placed on each believer's life. Christians face various challenges and temptations that can test their faith and commitment. However, determination helps them stay focused on their spiritual goals and persevere through difficulties.

In both NASCAR and the Christian life, determination involves setting clear goals and working tirelessly to achieve them. NASCAR drivers set goals for each race, aiming to improve their lap times, master specific tracks, and ultimately win championships. They develop detailed plans and strategies, continually refining their approach to maximize their performance. Similarly, Christians set spiritual goals, such as growing in their knowledge of God's Word, developing a deeper prayer life, and serving others with love and compassion. By setting these goals and diligently working toward them, believers can grow in their faith and make a positive impact in their communities.

Determination also involves resilience and the ability to bounce back from setbacks. In NASCAR, drivers often face crashes, mechanical failures, and other challenges that can hinder their progress. However, their determination drives them to recover quickly, learn from their experiences, and get back on the track. This resilience is a key component of their success. Similarly, Christians encounter setbacks and failures in their spiritual journey, but determination helps them rise again, seek God's forgiveness, and continue striving to follow Christ. Proverbs 24:16 highlights this resilience: "For a just man falleth seven times, and riseth up again: but the wicked shall fall into mischief." By maintaining a determined spirit, believers can overcome obstacles and grow stronger in their faith.

In both NASCAR and the Christian life, determination requires discipline and self-control. NASCAR drivers must maintain a strict regimen of physical training, mental preparation, and practice to stay competitive. They need to be disciplined in their diet, exercise, and rest to ensure they are in peak condition for races. Similarly, Christians are called to exercise spiritual discipline through regular prayer, Bible study, worship, and fellowship with other believers. These spiritual disciplines help believers stay focused on their relationship with God and build the strength and resilience needed to navigate life's challenges. 1 Corinthians 9:25-27 illustrates the importance of discipline: "And every man that striveth for the mastery is temperate in all things. Now they do it to obtain a corruptible crown; but we an incorruptible. I therefore so run, not as uncertainly; so fight I, not as one that beateth the air: But I keep under my body, and bring it into subjection: lest that by any means, when I have preached to others, I myself should be a castaway."

Another crucial aspect of determination is the support and encouragement from others. In NASCAR, drivers rely on their pit crew, engineers, and support staff to provide the necessary assistance and motivation to succeed. This teamwork and collaboration are vital for achieving their goals. Similarly, Christians benefit from the support and encouragement of their fellow believers. The Christian community provides a network of support through prayer, accountability, and mutual encouragement. Hebrews 10:2425 encourages believers to support one another: "And let us consider one another to provoke unto love and to good works: Not forsaking the assembling of ourselves together, as the manner of some is; but exhorting one another: and so much the more, as ye see the day approaching." By supporting and encouraging each other, believers can stay determined in their walk with Christ.

Determination also involves a strong sense of purpose and direction. NASCAR drivers have a clear goal of winning races and championships, and this goal drives their efforts and determination. Similarly, Christians have a clear purpose of glorifying God and fulfilling His calling on their lives. This purpose provides direction and motivation, helping believers stay focused and determined in their spiritual journey. Ephesians 2:10 reminds believers of their purpose: "For we are his workmanship, created in Christ Jesus unto good works, which God hath before ordained that we should walk in them." Understanding and embracing this purpose helps Christians stay determined in their efforts to follow Christ and make a powerful impact in the world with the work and Word of God.

In both NASCAR and the Christian life, determination requires perseverance through challenges and trials. NASCAR drivers face numerous obstacles, such as tough competition, adverse weather conditions, and physical and mental fatigue. Their determination drives them to persevere through these challenges and keep pushing toward their goals. Similarly, Christians face trials and temptations that can test their faith and commitment. However, determination helps them persevere, trusting in God's strength and guidance. James 1:12 encourages believers to persevere: "Blessed is the man that endureth temptation: for when he is tried, he shall receive the crown of life, which the Lord hath promised to them that love him." By persevering through challenges, Christians can grow stronger in their faith and experience the blessings of God's promises.

Determination also involves maintaining a positive attitude and outlook. NASCAR drivers who stay positive and focused on their goals are more likely to overcome setbacks and perform well. This positive mindset helps them stay motivated and resilient. Similarly, Christians are called to maintain a Christlike attitude, trusting in God's goodness and promises. Philippians 4:13 provides encouragement: "I can do all things through Christ which strengtheneth me." By focusing on God's strength and promises, believers can stay determined and motivated in their spiritual journey.

Another important aspect of determination is the willingness to make sacrifices. NASCAR drivers often make significant personal sacrifices, such as time away from family, rigorous training schedules, and financial investments, to pursue their racing careers. These sacrifices are driven by their determination to succeed. Similarly, Christians are called to make sacrifices in their pursuit of following Christ. This may involve giving up certain comforts, prioritizing time for spiritual practices, and serving others selflessly. Romans 12:1 encourages believers to present their bodies as a living sacrifice: "I beseech you therefore, brethren, by the mercies of God, that ye present your bodies a living sacrifice, holy, acceptable unto God, which is your reasonable service." These sacrifices, driven by determination, help believers grow in their faith and fulfill God's purposes.

In conclusion, determination is a crucial trait in both NASCAR and the Christian life, driving individuals to pursue their goals with relentless effort and unwavering focus. NASCAR drivers are determined to win, putting in countless hours of training, practice, and preparation to improve their skills and enhance their performance on the track. Similarly, Christians are called to be determined in their pursuit of following Christ, pressing forward with purpose and resolve to fulfill God's calling on their lives. Philippians 3:14 encapsulates this determination: "I press toward the mark for the prize of the high calling of God in Christ Jesus." By setting clear goals, maintaining discipline, relying on support from others, embracing their purpose, persevering through challenges, maintaining a positive attitude, and making necessary sacrifices, both NASCAR drivers and Christians can stay determined and achieve their desired outcomes. This determination not only helps individuals succeed in their respective pursuits but also brings glory to God and fulfills His purposes for their lives.

Chapter 16 Victory Celebration

VICTORY CELEBRATIONS are a significant aspect of both NASCAR and the Christian life, as they represent the culmination of hard work, perseverance, and dedication. In NASCAR, winners celebrate their victory with great enthusiasm and joy. After crossing the finish line first, drivers often perform celebratory burnouts, spin their cars in circles, and wave to the cheering crowd. They might climb out of their cars, pump their fists in the air, and hug their team members. These moments are filled with elation and pride, as the driver and their team acknowledge the effort and teamwork that led to their success. Victory lane becomes a hub of activity, with photographers capturing the moment, team members spraying champagne, and the winning driver holding the trophy high. Fans join in the celebration, cheering for their favorite driver and sharing in the excitement. These victory celebrations are not just about the driver but about the entire team, as each member played a crucial role in achieving the win. The celebrations also extend beyond the track, with media interviews, social media posts, and special events highlighting the triumph. These moments of victory are cherished memories that motivate drivers and teams to continue striving for excellence.

Similarly, Christians look forward to a victory celebration in heaven that will surpass any earthly celebration. This ultimate victory celebration is promised to those who have remained faithful to God and have persevered through the trials and challenges of life. Revelation 21:4 describes the joy and peace of this heavenly celebration: "And God shall wipe away all tears from their eyes; and there shall be no more death, neither sorrow, nor crying, neither shall there be any more pain: for the former things are passed away." This verse paints a picture of a place where all suffering and pain are gone, replaced by eternal joy and peace in the presence of God. For Christians, this heavenly celebration represents the fulfillment of God's promises and the reward for their faithfulness.

In the Christian life, the anticipation of this ultimate victory celebration provides hope and encouragement. Just as NASCAR drivers push through challenges with the hope of celebrating in victory lane, Christians persevere through life's difficulties with the assurance of a future celebration in heaven. This hope helps believers stay focused on their spiritual journey, knowing that their efforts and sacrifices are not in vain. It also provides comfort during times of sorrow and loss, as Christians look forward to the day when God will wipe away every tear and remove all pain.

Both NASCAR victory celebrations and the Christian hope of heaven involve a sense of community and shared joy. In NASCAR, the entire team shares in the victory celebration, recognizing that each member's contributions were essential to the win. Similarly, the heavenly celebration will be a communal event, where believers from all generations and backgrounds come together to rejoice in God's presence. This sense of unity and shared joy is a powerful reminder of the importance of community and fellowship in the Christian life. Hebrews 10:24-25 encourages believers to support and encourage one another: "And let us consider one another to provoke unto love and to good works: Not forsaking the assembling of ourselves together, as the manner of some is; but exhorting one another: and so much the more, as ye see the day approaching." By fostering a strong sense of community and supporting each other, Christians can help one another stay focused on the ultimate victory celebration in heaven.

The preparations for a NASCAR victory celebration begin long before the race day. Teams work tirelessly to prepare the car, strategize for the race, and ensure everything is in place for a successful performance. Similarly, Christians prepare for the heavenly celebration through their faith, obedience, and service. This preparation involves regular prayer, studying God's Word, participating in worship, and serving others with love and compassion. These spiritual disciplines help believers grow in their faith and stay connected to God, ensuring they are ready for the ultimate victory celebration.

In both NASCAR and the Christian life, the journey to victory is marked by perseverance and overcoming obstacles. NASCAR drivers face intense competition, challenging track conditions, and the ever-present risk of accidents. Despite these challenges, their determination and hard work drive them to keep pushing forward. Similarly, Christians face various trials and temptations that test their faith and commitment. James 1:12 offers encouragement to those who persevere: "Blessed is the man that endureth temptation: for when he is tried, he shall receive the crown of life, which the Lord hath promised to them that love him." By remaining steadfast in their faith and trusting in God's promises, believers can look forward to the ultimate victory celebration in heaven.

The joy and excitement of a NASCAR victory celebration are a reflection of the deeper joy that Christians will experience in heaven. While the celebrations on earth are temporary and fleeting, the joy of heaven is eternal and unending. This eternal joy is rooted in the presence of God, who is the source of all goodness and happiness. Revelation 21:3 provides a glimpse of this eternal joy: "And I heard a great voice out of heaven saying, Behold, the tabernacle of God is with men, and he will dwell with them, and they shall be his people, and God himself shall be with them, and be their God." The promise of God's presence and the absence of pain and suffering make the heavenly celebration the ultimate fulfillment of every believer's deepest desires.

In NASCAR, victory celebrations also serve as a motivation for future races. The taste of victory inspires drivers and teams to continue striving for excellence, pushing themselves to achieve even greater success. Similarly, the hope of the heavenly celebration motivates Christians to live faithfully and serve diligently. The anticipation of eternal joy and peace with God encourages believers to keep pressing forward, even when the journey is difficult. Philippians 3:13-14 captures this forward-looking determination: "Brethren, I count not myself to have apprehended: but this one thing I do, forgetting those things which are behind, and reaching forth unto those things which are before, I press toward the mark for the prize of the high calling of God in Christ Jesus." This verse emphasizes the importance of keeping our eyes on the prize and striving toward the ultimate victory celebration.

Both NASCAR victory celebrations and the Christian hope of heaven involve gratitude and recognition. In NASCAR, drivers often express gratitude to their teams, sponsors, and fans for their support and contributions to the victory. Similarly, Christians will express gratitude to God for His grace, love, and faithfulness. The heavenly celebration will be a time of worship and thanksgiving, where believers acknowledge God's goodness and give Him the glory for their salvation. Revelation 7:9-10 describes a scene of worship in heaven: "After this I beheld, and, lo, a great multitude, which no man could number, of all nations, and kindreds, and people, and tongues, stood before the throne, and before the Lamb, clothed with white robes, and palms in their hands; And cried with a loud voice, saying, Salvation to our God which sitteth upon the throne, and unto the Lamb." This scene highlights the importance of gratitude and worship in the ultimate victory celebration.

In conclusion, victory celebrations are a significant aspect of both NASCAR and the Christian life, representing the culmination of hard work, perseverance, and dedication. In NASCAR, winners celebrate their victory with great enthusiasm, acknowledging the effort and teamwork that led to their success. Similarly, Christians look forward to a victory celebration in heaven, where all suffering and pain will be gone, replaced by eternal joy and peace in the presence of God. Revelation 21:4 describes this heavenly celebration: "And God shall wipe away all tears from their eyes; and there shall be no more death, neither sorrow, nor crying, neither shall there be any more pain: for the former things are passed away." By maintaining a strong sense of community, preparing diligently, persevering through challenges, and expressing gratitude, both NASCAR drivers and Christians can look forward to their respective victory celebrations with hope and anticipation. The ultimate victory celebration in heaven is the fulfillment of God's promises and the reward for a life lived faithfully in His service.

Chapter 17 Navigating Obstacles

Navigating obstacles is a crucial part of both NASCAR and the Christian life, as drivers and believers alike must face and overcome various challenges to reach their goals. In NASCAR, drivers navigate through obstacles on the track, such as sharp turns, high speeds, and potential collisions with other cars. The track itself can present numerous hazards, including slick surfaces, debris, and varying weather conditions that can affect visibility and traction. Drivers must remain focused, alert, and adaptable to maneuver their cars safely and efficiently through these obstacles. This requires a combination of skill, quick reflexes, and strategic thinking. Each race demands that drivers constantly assess their surroundings, make split-second decisions, and anticipate the movements of other drivers to avoid crashes and maintain their position. The pit crew also plays a vital role, making crucial adjustments and repairs to ensure the car is in optimal condition to handle the track's challenges. Success in NASCAR is not just about speed but also about the ability to navigate obstacles effectively and consistently.

Similarly, Christians navigate through life's challenges, relying on their faith and trust in God to guide them through difficult times. Life is filled with various obstacles, such as personal struggles, relationship issues, financial difficulties, health problems, and societal pressures. These challenges can be overwhelming and may test a person's faith and resolve. However, Christians are encouraged to trust in God's presence and promises as they navigate these obstacles. Isaiah 43:2 offers reassurance: "When thou passest through the waters, I will be with thee; and through the rivers, they shall not overflow thee: when thou walkest through the fire, thou shalt not be burned; neither shall the flame kindle upon thee." This verse highlights God's commitment to being with His people through all trials, providing strength and protection as they face life's challenges.

In both NASCAR and the Christian life, preparation and training are essential for successfully navigating obstacles. NASCAR drivers undergo extensive training to develop their driving skills, improve their reaction times, and learn how to handle their cars in various conditions. They study the tracks, analyze previous races, and work with their teams to devise strategies for each race. This preparation helps them anticipate potential obstacles and respond effectively when they arise. Similarly, Christians prepare for life's challenges through spiritual disciplines such as prayer, Bible study, worship, and fellowship with other believers. These practices help build a strong foundation of faith, providing the wisdom and strength needed to navigate obstacles. Psalm 119:105 says, "Thy word is a lamp unto my feet, and a light unto my path," emphasizing the importance of God's Word in guiding believers through life's challenges.

Both NASCAR drivers and Christians must also be adaptable and flexible in their approach to navigating obstacles. On the racetrack, conditions can change rapidly, requiring drivers to adjust their strategies and make quick decisions. Whether it's a sudden change in weather, an unexpected move by a competitor, or a mechanical issue, drivers must be ready to adapt to the situation and find the best way forward. Similarly, Christians must be adaptable in their spiritual journey, ready to adjust their plans and approaches as they seek God's guidance. Proverbs 3:5-6 encourages believers to trust in God's direction: "Trust in the LORD with all thine heart; and lean not unto thine own understanding. In all thy ways acknowledge him, and he shall direct thy paths." By being flexible and open to God's leading, Christians can navigate life's challenges more effectively.

Resilience is another crucial aspect of navigating obstacles in both NASCAR and the Christian life. NASCAR drivers often face crashes, mechanical failures, and other setbacks that can hinder their progress. Their resilience drives them to recover quickly, learn from their experiences, and get back on the track. This resilience is a key component of their success. Similarly, Christians encounter setbacks and failures in their spiritual journey, but resilience helps them rise again, seek God's forgiveness, and continue striving to follow Christ. James 1:2-4 highlights the importance of resilience: "My brethren, count it all joy when ye fall into divers temptations; Knowing this, that the trying of your faith worketh patience. But let patience have her perfect work, that ye may be perfect and entire, wanting nothing." By maintaining a resilient spirit, believers can overcome obstacles and grow stronger in their faith.

Support from others is also vital for navigating obstacles. In NASCAR, drivers rely on their pit crews, engineers, and support staff to provide the necessary assistance and motivation to succeed. This teamwork and collaboration are essential for overcoming challenges and achieving their goals. Similarly, Christians benefit from the support and encouragement of their fellow believers. The Christian community provides a network of support through prayer, accountability, and mutual encouragement. Hebrews 10:2425 encourages believers to support one another: "And let us consider one another to provoke unto love and to good works: Not forsaking the assembling of ourselves together, as the manner of some is; but exhorting one another: and so much the more, as ye see the day approaching." By supporting and encouraging each other, believers can navigate life's obstacles with greater strength and resilience.

In both NASCAR and the Christian life, determination and perseverance are key to navigating obstacles. NASCAR drivers face numerous challenges, such as tough competition, adverse weather conditions, and physical and mental fatigue. Their determination and perseverance drive them to push through these challenges and keep striving for victory. Similarly, Christians face trials and temptations that can test their faith and commitment. However, determination and perseverance help them press on, trusting in God's strength and guidance. Philippians 3:13-14 captures this forward looking determination: "Brethren, I count not myself to have apprehended: but this one thing I do, forgetting those things which are behind, and reaching forth unto those things which are before, I press toward the mark for the prize of the high calling of God in Christ Jesus." By keeping their eyes on the ultimate goal and persevering through challenges, Christians can navigate life's obstacles with confidence and hope.

Another important aspect of navigating obstacles is maintaining a positive attitude and perspective. NASCAR drivers who stay positive and focused on their goals are more likely to overcome setbacks and perform well. This positive mindset helps them stay motivated and resilient. Similarly, Christians are called to maintain a positive attitude, trusting in God's goodness and promises. Philippians 4:13 provides encouragement: "I can do all things through Christ which strengtheneth me." By focusing on God's strength and promises, believers can stay determined and motivated in their spiritual journey.

In conclusion, navigating obstacles is a crucial part of both NASCAR and the Christian life, as drivers and believers alike must face and overcome various challenges to reach their goals. NASCAR drivers navigate through obstacles on the track, such as sharp turns, high speeds, and potential collisions, relying on their skills, training, and teamwork to succeed. Similarly, Christians navigate through life's challenges by trusting in God's presence and promises, engaging in spiritual disciplines, and relying on the support and encouragement of their fellow believers. Isaiah 43:2 offers reassurance of God's presence through all trials: "When thou passest through the waters, I will be with thee; and through the rivers, they shall not overflow thee: when thou walkest through the fire, thou shalt not be burned; neither shall the flame kindle upon thee." By maintaining resilience, adaptability, determination, and a positive attitude, both NASCAR drivers and Christians can navigate obstacles effectively and continue striving toward their ultimate goals.

Chapter 18 Support Team

SUPPORT TEAMS ARE ESSENTIAL in both NASCAR and the Christian life, as they provide the necessary assistance, encouragement, and resources to help individuals succeed. In NASCAR, the team supporting the driver plays a crucial role in the success of the race. This team includes the pit crew, engineers, mechanics, strategists, and support staff who work together to ensure the car is in optimal condition and that the driver has everything needed to perform at their best. The pit crew is responsible for making quick tire changes, refueling the car, and performing any necessary repairs during pit stops. Their speed and efficiency can make a significant difference in the outcome of the race. Engineers and mechanics work behind the scenes to fine-tune the car, ensuring it can handle the rigors of high-speed racing. They analyze data from practice runs and previous races to make adjustments that will improve the car's performance. Strategists develop race plans, considering factors such as weather conditions, track characteristics, and the strengths and weaknesses of competitors. Communication is key, with the driver relying on the spotter to provide real-time updates about the position of other cars and any potential hazards on the track. The collective effort of the support team helps the driver navigate obstacles, make strategic decisions, and ultimately strive for victory. Without this support, the driver would be unable to compete effectively and safely.

Similarly, in the Christian life, the church serves as a support team for each member, providing spiritual guidance, encouragement, and practical help. The Bible emphasizes the importance of mutual support and encouragement among believers, as seen in Hebrews 10:24-25: "And let us consider one another to provoke unto love and to good works: Not forsaking the assembling of ourselves together, as the manner of some is; but exhorting one another: and so much the more, as ye see the day approaching." This verse highlights the need for Christians to gather together, support one another, and spur each other on to live out their faith. The church is a community of believers who come together to worship, pray, study God's Word, and serve others. Within this community, each member has a role to play, using their unique gifts and talents to contribute to the overall mission of the church.

In the church, pastors and spiritual leaders provide guidance and teaching, helping members grow in their understanding of God's Word and apply it to their lives. They offer counsel, encouragement, and support during times of difficulty, helping individuals navigate challenges and make wise decisions. Fellowship is another important aspect of the church's support system. Believers gather together for worship services, small group meetings, and other church activities, building relationships and creating a sense of belonging. These connections provide a network of support, allowing members to share their struggles, celebrate their victories, and encourage one another in their faith journey.

Prayer is a powerful way the church supports its members. Believers pray for each other's needs, intercede on behalf of those who are struggling, and seek God's guidance and strength together. James 5:16 emphasizes the importance of prayer: "Confess your faults one to another, and pray one for another, that ye may be healed. The effectual fervent prayer of a righteous man availeth much." Through prayer, the church can uplift and support its members, helping them experience God's presence and power in their lives.

Practical help and service are also key components of the church's support system. Just as the pit crew provides essential services to the NASCAR driver, church members offer practical assistance to those in need. This can include providing meals for families during times of illness or crisis, helping with household chores, offering transportation, or providing financial support. Acts 2:44-45 describes the early church's commitment to supporting one another: "And all that believed were together, and had all things common; And sold their possessions and goods, and parted them to all men, as every man had need." By meeting each other's practical needs, the church demonstrates the love and compassion of Christ and strengthens the bonds of community.

Encouragement and accountability are also vital aspects of the church's support system. Believers encourage one another to stay faithful to God's calling, pursue spiritual growth, and live out their faith in practical ways. This encouragement can come through personal conversations, small group discussions, or public recognition of individuals' efforts and achievements. Accountability involves holding one another responsible for their actions and decisions, offering loving correction when necessary, and helping each other stay on the right path. Proverbs 27:17 says, "Iron sharpeneth iron; so a man sharpeneth the countenance of his friend." By holding each other accountable, believers can grow stronger in their faith and avoid falling into sin.

Teaching and discipleship are critical components of the church's support system. Pastors, teachers, and mentors provide instruction in God's Word, helping members understand biblical truths and apply them to their lives. Discipleship involves walking alongside others in their faith journey, offering guidance, support, and encouragement as they grow in their relationship with God. This process of teaching and discipleship helps individuals develop a strong foundation of faith and equips them to navigate life's challenges with confidence.

In both NASCAR and the Christian life, the support team plays a vital role in helping individuals achieve their goals. NASCAR drivers rely on their team to provide the necessary support, guidance, and resources to perform at their best. Similarly, Christians rely on the church to provide spiritual support, encouragement, and practical help as they pursue their faith journey. The collective effort of the support team helps individuals overcome obstacles, make wise decisions, and stay focused on their goals.

Unity and cooperation are essential for the success of both NASCAR teams and the church. In NASCAR, the team's success depends on the ability of its members to work together seamlessly, communicate effectively, and support one another. Similarly, the church's effectiveness in fulfilling its mission depends on the unity and cooperation of its members. Ephesians 4:3 encourages believers to "endeavor to keep the unity of the Spirit in the bond of peace." By working together in unity and supporting one another, the church can accomplish great things and bring glory to God.

In conclusion, support teams are essential in both NASCAR and the Christian life, providing the necessary assistance, encouragement, and resources to help individuals succeed. In NASCAR, the team supporting the driver plays a crucial role in the success of the race, ensuring the car is in optimal condition and that the driver has everything needed to perform at their best. Similarly, the church serves as a support team for each member, providing spiritual guidance, encouragement, and practical help. Hebrews 10:24-25 highlights the importance of mutual support and encouragement among believers: "And let us consider one another to provoke unto love and to good works: Not forsaking the assembling of ourselves together, as the manner of some is; but exhorting one another: and so much the more, as ye see the day approaching." By providing spiritual guidance, practical help, encouragement, accountability, teaching, and discipleship, the church can support its members in their faith journey and help them achieve their spiritual goals. Unity and cooperation are essential for the success of both NASCAR teams and the church, as they enable individuals to work together seamlessly and accomplish great things.

Chapter 19 Rules

RULES ARE ESSENTIAL in both NASCAR and the Christian life, as they provide structure, guidance, and boundaries that help individuals achieve their goals while maintaining order and integrity. In NASCAR, drivers follow strict rules to ensure fair competition, safety, and the smooth operation of races. These rules cover various aspects of the sport, including car specifications, track regulations, race procedures, and driver conduct. NASCAR's governing body enforces these rules rigorously, with penalties for violations ranging from fines and point deductions to disqualification from races. For example, cars must meet specific technical standards, such as weight, engine size, and aerodynamic features, to ensure a level playing field. During races, drivers must adhere to rules regarding speed limits in pit lanes, the timing of pit stops, and overtaking other cars. Safety rules, such as wearing protective gear and following protocols for crashes and mechanical failures, protect drivers, crew members, and spectators. The rules also promote sportsmanship, requiring drivers to compete with respect and integrity. These rules are not arbitrary; they are designed to enhance the competition, ensure fairness, and protect everyone involved. By following these rules, drivers can focus on their performance and strategy, knowing that the race is conducted fairly and safely.

Similarly, in the Christian life, believers follow God's commandments, which provide moral and spiritual guidance for living a life that honors God and reflects His love. God's commandments are outlined in the Bible and include instructions on how to love and serve God, treat others, and live a righteous and holy life. John 14:21 emphasizes the importance of keeping God's commandments: "He that hath my commandments, and keepeth them, he it is that loveth me: and he that loveth me shall be loved of my Father, and I will love him, and will manifest myself to him." This verse highlights that obedience to God's commandments is an expression of love for Him and that it leads to a deeper relationship with God, who promises to reveal Himself to those who obey Him.

In both NASCAR and the Christian life, following rules requires discipline and commitment. NASCAR drivers must be disciplined in their adherence to the rules, understanding that violations can lead to penalties that affect their performance and standings. They must stay informed about any changes or updates to the rules and ensure that their team complies with all regulations. This discipline helps maintain the integrity of the sport and ensures that every driver competes under the same conditions. Similarly, Christians must be disciplined in their obedience to God's commandments, striving to live according to His Word and aligning their actions with His will. This requires regular study of the Bible, prayer, and reflection to understand God's instructions and apply them to daily life. By following God's commandments, believers demonstrate their commitment to Him and their desire to live a life that pleases Him.

Following rules in both NASCAR and the Christian life also involves accountability. In NASCAR, drivers, teams, and officials hold each other accountable for adhering to the rules. Race officials monitor the race closely, using technology and their expertise to identify any rule violations. When a driver or team member breaks a rule, they are held accountable through penalties, ensuring that everyone competes fairly. This accountability helps maintain the credibility and integrity of the sport. Similarly, in the Christian life, believers hold each other accountable for living according to God's commandments. This accountability occurs within the context of the church community, where fellow believers encourage, support, and sometimes correct each other to stay on the right path. Hebrews 10:24-25 highlights the importance of mutual accountability and encouragement: "And let us consider one another to provoke unto love and to good works: Not forsaking the assembling of ourselves together, as the manner of some is; but exhorting one another: and so much the more, as ye see the day approaching." By holding each other accountable, Christians help one another grow in their faith and maintain a life of obedience to God.

Both NASCAR and the Christian life recognize that rules are not meant to be burdensome but are designed to promote well-being, fairness, and success. In NASCAR, the rules ensure that all drivers have an equal opportunity to compete, that races are conducted safely, and that the sport remains enjoyable for fans and participants. These rules create a structured environment where drivers can focus on their skills, strategies, and teamwork without worrying about unfair advantages or unsafe conditions. Similarly, God's commandments are given for the benefit of believers, guiding them toward a life of righteousness, peace, and fulfillment. God's rules help protect individuals from the consequences of sin, promote healthy relationships, and lead to a deeper understanding of His love and purpose for their lives. Psalm

19:7-8 describes the value of God's commandments: "The law of the LORD is perfect, converting the soul: the testimony of the LORD is sure, making wise the simple. The statutes of the LORD are right, rejoicing the heart: the commandment of the LORD is pure, enlightening the eyes." By following God's commandments, believers can experience the joy, wisdom, and peace that come from living in alignment with His will.

In both NASCAR and the Christian life, rules serve as a foundation for growth and improvement. NASCAR drivers and teams continuously strive to improve their performance within the framework of the rules. They use the rules as guidelines for innovation, finding ways to enhance their cars' speed, handling, and efficiency while staying within the regulations. This pursuit of excellence drives technological advancements and pushes the boundaries of the sport. Similarly, Christians use God's commandments as a foundation for spiritual growth. By studying and obeying God's Word, believers can deepen their understanding of His character, grow in their faith, and develop a closer relationship with Him. This ongoing process of growth and transformation is guided by the principles and instructions found in the Bible. 2 Timothy 3:16-17 emphasizes the role of Scripture in guiding believers: "All scripture is given by inspiration of God, and is profitable for doctrine, for reproof, for correction, for instruction in righteousness: That the man of God may be perfect, thoroughly furnished unto all good works." By following God's commandments, Christians can grow in their faith and become more effective in living out their calling.

Obedience to rules in both NASCAR and the Christian life also brings a sense of order and stability. In NASCAR, the rules ensure that races are conducted in an orderly manner, with clear guidelines for drivers and teams to follow. This orderliness helps prevent chaos and confusion, allowing races to proceed smoothly and safely. Similarly, God's commandments provide a sense of order and stability in the lives of believers. By following God's instructions, Christians can navigate the complexities of life with confidence, knowing that they are guided by divine wisdom. This sense of order helps believers make wise decisions, build healthy relationships, and live with purpose and direction. Proverbs 3:5-6 encourages believers to trust in God's guidance: "Trust in the LORD with all thine heart; and lean not unto thine own understanding. In all thy ways acknowledge him, and he shall direct thy paths." By trusting in God's commandments, Christians can experience the peace and stability that come from living in alignment with His will.

In both NASCAR and the Christian life, rules help build a sense of community and shared values. NASCAR drivers, teams, and fans are united by their commitment to the sport's rules and principles. This shared commitment fosters a sense of camaraderie, respect, and mutual support among participants and spectators. Similarly, God's commandments create a sense of community among believers, who are united by their shared faith and commitment to living according to God's Word. This unity is expressed through worship, fellowship, and acts of service, as believers come together to support and encourage one another in their spiritual journey. Ephesians 4:1-3 emphasizes the importance of unity among believers: "I therefore, the prisoner of the Lord, beseech you that ye walk worthy of the vocation wherewith ye are called, With all lowliness and meekness, with longsuffering, forbearing one another in love; Endeavoring to keep the unity of the Spirit in the bond of peace." By following God's commandments, Christians can build a strong, unified community that reflects God's love and grace to the world.

In conclusion, rules are essential in both NASCAR and the Christian life, providing structure, guidance, and boundaries that help individuals achieve their goals while maintaining order and integrity. In NASCAR, drivers follow strict rules to ensure fair competition, safety, and the smooth operation of races. These rules cover various aspects of the sport, including car specifications, track regulations, race procedures, and driver conduct. Similarly, in the Christian life, believers follow God's commandments, which provide moral and spiritual guidance for living a life that honors God and reflects His love. John 14:21 emphasizes the importance of keeping God's commandments: "He that hath my commandments, and keepeth them, he it is that loveth me: and he that loveth me shall be loved of my Father, and I will love him, and will manifest myself to him." By following rules in both NASCAR and the Christian life, individuals can experience the benefits of discipline, accountability, growth, order, and community, ultimately achieving their goals and fulfilling their purposes.

Chapter 20 Pit Crew

THE PIT CREW IS ESSENTIAL in NASCAR and the Christian life because they provide critical support and assistance to the driver and fellow believers. In NASCAR, the pit crew helps the driver during the race by performing quick and efficient pit stops. These stops include changing tires, refueling the car, making mechanical adjustments, and addressing any issues that arise during the race. The pit crew's speed, skill, and coordination can make the difference between winning and losing, as they ensure that the car remains in optimal condition and that the driver can return to the track as quickly as possible. Each member of the pit crew has a specific role, such as tire changer, fueler, jackman, and crew chief, and they must work together seamlessly to achieve their common goal. Their efforts are characterized by precision, teamwork, and dedication, reflecting hours of practice and preparation. The success of the driver is heavily dependent on the pit crew's performance, highlighting the importance of each member's contribution to the overall team effort. This dynamic mirrors the Christian life, where fellow believers help and encourage each other, providing spiritual and practical support to navigate life's challenges.

In the Christian life, fellow believers act as a pit crew for one another, bearing each other's burdens and offering support, encouragement, and guidance. Galatians 6:2 emphasizes this role: "Bear ye one another's burdens, and so fulfil the law of Christ." This verse highlights the importance of mutual support within the Christian community, where believers come together to share their struggles, joys, and responsibilities. Just as a NASCAR driver relies on their pit crew for assistance, Christians rely on their spiritual family to help them grow in faith, overcome obstacles, and stay focused on their journey with God. This support can take many forms, including prayer, counseling, fellowship, and acts of service, all aimed at strengthening the bonds of love and unity within the church.

Prayer is a powerful way believers support one another, similar to how the pit crew communicates with the driver to provide updates and guidance. Christians pray for each other's needs, intercede on behalf of those facing difficulties, and seek God's wisdom and strength together. James 5:16 underscores the importance of prayer: "Confess your faults one to another, and pray one for another, that ye may be healed. The effectual fervent prayer of a righteous man availeth much." Through prayer, believers can uplift and support each other, helping to bear one another's burdens and experience God's presence and power in their lives.

Fellowship is another crucial aspect of the Christian support system, akin to the camaraderie and teamwork seen in a NASCAR pit crew. Believers gather together for worship services, small group meetings, and other church activities, building relationships and creating a sense of belonging. These connections provide a network of support, allowing members to share their struggles, celebrate their victories, and encourage one another in their faith journey. Hebrews 10:24-25 encourages believers to support one another: "And let us consider one another to provoke unto love and to good works: Not forsaking the assembling of ourselves together, as the manner of some is; but exhorting one another: and so much the more, as ye see the day approaching." By fostering a strong sense of community and supporting each other, Christians can help one another stay focused on their spiritual goals and navigate the challenges of life.

Acts of service are also vital in the Christian community, reflecting the practical assistance provided by the pit crew during a race. Believers offer practical help to those in need, such as providing meals, helping with household chores, offering transportation, or providing financial support. Acts 2:44-45 describes the early church's commitment to supporting one another: "And all that believed were together, and had all things common; And sold their possessions and goods, and parted them to all men, as every man had need." By meeting each other's practical needs, the church demonstrates the love and compassion of Christ and strengthens the bonds of community.

Encouragement and accountability are essential components of the Christian support system, much like the pit crew's role in motivating and guiding the driver. Believers encourage one another to stay faithful to God's calling, pursue spiritual growth, and live out their faith in practical ways. This encouragement can come through personal conversations, small group discussions, or public recognition of individuals' efforts and achievements. Accountability involves holding one another responsible for their actions and decisions, offering loving correction when necessary, and helping each other stay on the right path. Proverbs 27:17 says, "Iron sharpeneth iron; so a man sharpeneth the countenance of his friend." By holding each other accountable, believers can grow stronger in their faith and avoid falling into sin.

Teaching and discipleship are critical components of the Christian support system, similar to how the pit crew provides guidance and instruction to the driver. Pastors, teachers, and mentors provide instruction in God's Word, helping members understand biblical truths and apply them to their lives. Discipleship involves walking alongside others in their faith journey, offering guidance, support, and encouragement as they grow in their relationship with God. This process of teaching and discipleship helps individuals develop a strong foundation of faith and equips them to navigate life's challenges with confidence. 2 Timothy 3:16-17 emphasizes the role of Scripture in guiding believers: "All scripture is given by inspiration of God, and is profitable for doctrine, for reproof, for correction, for instruction in righteousness: That the man of God may be perfect, thoroughly furnished unto all good works." By following God's commandments, Christians can grow in their faith and become more effective in living out their calling.

Unity and cooperation are essential for the success of both a NASCAR pit crew and the Christian community. In NASCAR, the team's success depends on the ability of its members to work together seamlessly, communicate effectively, and support one another. Similarly, the church's effectiveness in fulfilling its mission depends on the unity and cooperation of its members. Ephesians 4:3 encourages believers to "endeavor to keep the unity of the Spirit in the bond of peace." By working together in unity and supporting one another, the church can accomplish great things and bring glory to God.

In both NASCAR and the Christian life, the pit crew and fellow believers play a vital role in helping individuals achieve their goals. NASCAR drivers rely on their pit crew to provide the necessary support, guidance, and resources to perform at their best. Similarly, Christians rely on the church to provide spiritual support, encouragement, and practical help as they pursue their faith journey. The collective effort of the support team helps individuals overcome obstacles, make wise decisions, and stay focused on their goals.

The success of a NASCAR driver and a Christian depends heavily on the support they receive from their pit crew and fellow believers. Just as the pit crew's performance can make or break a race, the encouragement and support from the church community can significantly impact a believer's spiritual growth and resilience. Both require a high level of trust, communication, and commitment to a common goal.

In conclusion, the pit crew is essential in both NASCAR and the Christian life, providing critical support and assistance to the driver and fellow believers. In NASCAR, the pit crew helps the driver during the race by performing quick and efficient pit stops, ensuring the car remains in optimal condition and that the driver can return to the track as quickly as possible. Similarly, in the Christian life, fellow believers act as a pit crew for one another, bearing each other's burdens and offering support, encouragement, and guidance. Galatians 6:2 emphasizes this role: "Bear ye one another's burdens, and so fulfil the law of Christ." By providing spiritual guidance, practical help, encouragement, accountability, teaching, and discipleship, the church can support its members in their faith journey and help them achieve their spiritual goals. Unity and cooperation are essential for the success of both a NASCAR pit crew and the Christian community, as they enable individuals to work together seamlessly and accomplish great things.

Chapter 21 Race Course

THE RACE COURSE IN NASCAR is a carefully designed and challenging path that drivers must navigate to compete effectively, just as Christians run the race of faith on a course set before them by God. In NASCAR, each race takes place on a specific course, which can vary greatly in length, layout, and difficulty. Some courses are ovals, where drivers race around a track with long straightaways and high-banked turns, while others are road courses with a mix of tight corners, elevation changes, and straight sections. Drivers must familiarize themselves with each course, learning its unique characteristics and developing strategies to handle its challenges. They study the track layout, practice on the course, and work with their teams to fine-tune their cars for optimal performance. This preparation is crucial, as the ability to navigate the course effectively can mean the difference between winning and losing. During the race, drivers must stay focused, make quick decisions, and adapt to changing conditions, such as weather, track surface, and the actions of other drivers. The race course tests their skills, endurance, and mental toughness, requiring them to push their limits and strive for excellence.

Similarly, in the Christian life, believers run the race of faith on a course set before them by God. This spiritual race involves following God's path, overcoming obstacles, and striving to grow in faith and character. Hebrews 12:1 encourages Christians to run this race with perseverance: "Wherefore seeing we also are compassed about with so great a cloud of witnesses, let us lay aside every weight, and the sin which doth so easily beset us, and let us run with patience the race that is set before us." This verse reminds believers that they are surrounded by a community of faith, both past and present, who support and encourage them. It also emphasizes the importance of shedding distractions and sins that hinder their progress, allowing them to focus on the race with determination and patience.

In both NASCAR and the Christian life, preparation is key to navigating the race course successfully. NASCAR drivers prepare by studying the track, practicing their driving skills, and working with their teams to fine-tune their cars. Similarly, Christians prepare for their spiritual race through prayer, Bible study, worship, and fellowship with other believers. These spiritual disciplines help them grow in their knowledge of God, strengthen their faith, and equip them to face the challenges of life. Just as a driver must understand the nuances of a race track, Christians must understand God's Word and apply it to their lives, allowing it to guide their decisions and actions.

Both NASCAR drivers and Christians must stay focused on their course, avoiding distractions that can lead them astray. On the race track, drivers must maintain their concentration, keeping their eyes on the road and their minds on their strategy. They must avoid unnecessary risks and stay aware of their surroundings to navigate the course safely and effectively. Similarly, Christians must keep their focus on their faith journey, avoiding distractions that can lead them away from God. This involves being mindful of the influences in their lives, making choices that align with their faith, and staying committed to their spiritual goals. Proverbs 4:25-27 advises, "Let thine eyes look right on, and let thine eyelids look straight before thee. Ponder the path of thy feet, and let all thy ways be established. Turn not to the right hand nor to the left: remove thy foot from evil." By staying focused on their course, Christians can navigate their spiritual journey with integrity and purpose.

Perseverance is another essential quality for both NASCAR drivers and Christians as they navigate their respective courses. In NASCAR, drivers face numerous challenges, such as mechanical failures, accidents, and intense competition. Despite these obstacles, they must persevere, staying determined and resilient to reach the finish line.

This perseverance is fueled by their passion for the sport, their commitment to their team, and their desire to achieve their goals. Similarly, Christians face trials and temptations that can test their faith and resolve. James 1:12 encourages believers to persevere: "Blessed is the man that endureth temptation: for when he is tried, he shall receive the crown of life, which the Lord hath promised to them that love him." By persevering through difficulties, Christians grow stronger in their faith and develop a deeper reliance on God.

In both NASCAR and the Christian life, support from others is crucial for navigating the race course. NASCAR drivers rely on their pit crews, engineers, and spotters to provide the necessary support, guidance, and assistance during the race. This teamwork and collaboration are essential for overcoming challenges and achieving success. Similarly, Christians rely on the support and encouragement of their fellow believers. The Christian community provides a network of support through prayer, accountability, and mutual encouragement. Hebrews 10:24-25 highlights the importance of this support: "And let us consider one another to provoke unto love and to good works: Not forsaking the assembling of ourselves together, as the manner of some is; but exhorting one another: and so much the more, as ye see the day approaching." By supporting and encouraging each other, believers can navigate their spiritual race with greater strength and resilience.

Adaptability is also essential for both NASCAR drivers and Christians as they navigate their courses. On the race track, conditions can change rapidly, requiring drivers to adjust their strategies and make quick decisions. Whether it's a sudden change in weather, an unexpected move by a competitor, or a mechanical issue, drivers must be ready to adapt and find the best way forward. Similarly, Christians must be adaptable in their spiritual journey, ready to adjust their plans and approaches as they seek God's guidance. Proverbs 3:5-6 encourages believers to trust in God's direction: "Trust in the LORD with all thine heart; and lean not unto thine own understanding. In all thy ways acknowledge him, and he shall direct thy paths." By being flexible and open to God's leading, Christians can navigate their spiritual race more effectively.

Both NASCAR drivers and Christians must also set their sights on the ultimate goal, keeping their eyes on the prize. In NASCAR, the goal is to cross the finish line first, achieving victory and earning points toward the championship. This goal drives drivers to push their limits, stay focused, and persevere through challenges. Similarly, Christians run their race with the ultimate goal of eternal life with God. Philippians 3:13-14 captures this forward-looking determination: "Brethren, I count not myself to have apprehended: but this one thing I do, forgetting those things which are behind, and reaching forth unto those things which are before, I press toward the mark for the prize of the high calling of God in Christ Jesus." By keeping their eyes on the ultimate prize, Christians can stay motivated and committed to their faith journey.

Resilience is another important quality for navigating the race course in both NASCAR and the Christian life. NASCAR drivers often face crashes, mechanical failures, and other setbacks that can hinder their progress. Their resilience drives them to recover quickly, learn from their experiences, and get back on the track. This resilience is a key component of their success. Similarly, Christians encounter setbacks and failures in their spiritual journey, but resilience helps them rise again, seek God's forgiveness, and continue striving to follow Christ. Proverbs 24:16 highlights this resilience: "For a just man falleth seven times, and riseth up again: but the wicked shall fall into mischief." By maintaining a resilient spirit, believers can overcome obstacles and grow stronger in their faith.

In both NASCAR and the Christian life, the race course serves as a metaphor for the journey of growth, challenge, and perseverance. The race course in NASCAR is a tangible, physical path that drivers navigate with skill and determination. The race of faith for Christians is a spiritual journey that requires similar qualities of focus, perseverance, support, adaptability, and resilience. By understanding the parallels between these two races, believers can draw inspiration and strength from the lessons learned on the track and apply them to their spiritual journey.

In conclusion, the race course in NASCAR and the race of faith in the Christian life share many similarities, both requiring preparation, focus, perseverance, support, adaptability, and resilience. NASCAR drivers navigate their courses with skill and determination, relying on their teams and their own abilities to overcome challenges and strive for victory. Similarly, Christians navigate their spiritual race with faith and perseverance, relying on God's guidance and the support of their fellow believers to overcome obstacles and grow in their relationship with Him. Hebrews 12:1 encourages believers to run their race with perseverance: "Wherefore seeing we also are compassed about with so great a cloud of witnesses, let us lay aside every weight, and the sin which doth so easily beset us, and let us run with patience the race that is set before us." By applying these principles to their walk with God, Christians can navigate their race of faith with confidence and determination.

Chapter 22 The Checkered Flag

THE CHECKERED FLAG in NASCAR signals the end of the race, marking the culmination of intense competition, skillful driving, and strategic planning. It is the moment every driver strives for, representing the achievement of their goals and the reward for their hard work and perseverance. When a driver sees the checkered flag waving, it means they have completed the race, and if they are the first to cross the finish line, it signifies victory. The journey to the checkered flag is filled with challenges, including navigating through traffic, avoiding crashes, making quick decisions, and working closely with their team to ensure the car performs at its best. Each race is a test of endurance, skill, and mental toughness, and the checkered flag is the ultimate symbol of success and accomplishment in the sport of NASCAR.

Similarly, in the Christian life, the end of life on earth marks the beginning of eternity with Christ. This transition is the ultimate goal for believers, representing the completion of their earthly journey and the reward for their faithfulness and perseverance. Just as the checkered flag marks the end of a race and the beginning of a celebration, the end of a Christian's life on earth marks the beginning of eternal life with God, a time of joy and fulfillment beyond anything experienced in this world. 2 Timothy 4:7-8 captures this sentiment beautifully: "I have fought a good fight, I have finished my course, I have kept the faith: Henceforth there is laid up for me a crown of righteousness, which the Lord, the righteous judge, shall give me at that day: and not to me only, but unto all them also that love his appearing." This verse highlights the idea that life is a race, one that requires effort, dedication, and faith, and that finishing this race faithfully leads to a glorious reward.

In both NASCAR and the Christian life, reaching the end requires perseverance and determination. NASCAR drivers must maintain their focus and determination throughout the race, overcoming obstacles and staying committed to their strategy. They must push through fatigue, adapt to changing conditions, and keep their eyes on the goal. Similarly, Christians are called to persevere through life's challenges, maintaining their faith and commitment to God's path. This perseverance involves trusting in God's promises, staying strong in the face of trials, and continually striving to grow in their relationship with Him. James 1:12 encourages believers in this regard: "Blessed is the man that endureth temptation: for when he is tried, he shall receive the crown of life, which the Lord hath promised to them that love him." By persevering through difficulties and keeping their faith, Christians can look forward to the ultimate reward of eternal life with God.

Support and teamwork are crucial in both NASCAR and the Christian life. In NASCAR, drivers rely on their pit crews, spotters, and team members to help them navigate the race and reach the finish line. This support includes quick pit stops, strategic advice, and real-time information about the race conditions and competitors. The success of the driver is closely tied to the performance and coordination of the entire team. Similarly, Christians rely on the support of their fellow believers, the church community, and spiritual mentors to help them navigate their faith journey. This support includes prayer, encouragement, accountability, and guidance, all of which help believers stay on course and grow in their faith. Hebrews 10:24-25 emphasizes the importance of this support: "And let us consider one another to provoke unto love and to good works: Not forsaking the assembling of ourselves together, as the manner of some is; but exhorting one another: and so much the more, as ye see the day approaching." By supporting and encouraging one another, Christians can help each other stay strong and focused on their ultimate goal.

The checkered flag also represents a moment of reflection and celebration. For NASCAR drivers, crossing the finish line and seeing the checkered flag is a time to celebrate their hard work, the challenges they've overcome, and the success they've achieved. It's a moment to reflect on the race, the strategies that worked, and the teamwork that made it all possible. Similarly, the end of a Christian's life is a time of reflection on their faith journey, the ways they have grown, the challenges they have faced, and the faithfulness of God throughout it all. It's also a time of celebration, as believers look forward to the promise of eternal life with Christ. Revelation 21:4 describes this joyous transition: "And God shall wipe away all tears from their eyes; and there shall be no more death, neither sorrow, nor crying, neither shall there be any more pain: for the former things are passed away." The end of life on earth is not the end of the story but the beginning of a new and glorious chapter in eternity.

Just as the checkered flag signifies the end of one race and the preparation for the next, the end of a Christian's earthly life is the beginning of eternal life with God. This eternal life is the ultimate prize, far surpassing any earthly reward. It is a time of perfect peace, joy, and fulfillment in the presence of God. For believers, this promise of eternal life provides hope and motivation to keep running the race of faith with perseverance and dedication. Philippians 3:13-14 encourages believers to keep their eyes on this ultimate prize: "Brethren, I count not myself to have apprehended: but this one thing I do, forgetting those things which are behind, and reaching forth unto those things which are before, I press toward the mark for the prize of the high calling of God in Christ Jesus." By staying focused on the promise of eternity with God, Christians can find the strength and determination to overcome the challenges of this life and finish their race faithfully.

In both NASCAR and the Christian life, the journey to the checkered flag is filled with lessons and growth. NASCAR drivers learn from each race, gaining experience, improving their skills, and refining their strategies. They analyze their performance, learn from their mistakes, and continually strive to be better. Similarly, Christians grow and learn through their faith journey, gaining wisdom, deepening their understanding of God's Word, and becoming more like Christ. Each challenge and trial provides an opportunity for growth and transformation, helping believers to mature in their faith and draw closer to God. Romans 5:3-4 speaks to this process of growth: "And not only so, but we glory in tribulations also: knowing that tribulation worketh patience; And patience, experience; and experience, hope." By embracing the lessons and growth opportunities along the way, Christians can run their race with greater purpose and determination.

The checkered flag in NASCAR and the end of life for Christians also highlight the importance of finishing well. In NASCAR, it's not just about starting the race but about maintaining focus, determination, and skill to finish strong and cross the finish line successfully. Similarly, in the Christian life, it's important to run the race of faith with endurance and to finish well, remaining faithful to God until the end. This involves staying true to one's beliefs, continuing to grow in faith, and serving God faithfully throughout one's life. 2 Timothy 4:7-8 captures this desire to finish well: "I have fought a good fight, I have finished my course, I have kept the faith: Henceforth there is laid up for me a crown of righteousness, which the Lord, the righteous judge, shall give me at that day: and not to me only, but unto all them also that love his appearing." By striving to finish well, Christians can look forward to the ultimate reward of eternal life with God.

The checkered flag also symbolizes the transition from the temporary to the eternal. In NASCAR, the race is a temporary event, a moment in time where drivers compete for victory. The checkered flag marks the end of this temporary event and the beginning of the celebration and recognition of their achievement. Similarly, life on earth is temporary, a brief moment in the grand scheme of eternity.

The end of life marks the transition from this temporary existence to the eternal life promised by God. For believers, this transition is not something to be feared but something to be anticipated with hope and joy. John 14:2-3 provides comfort and assurance about this transition: "In my Father's house are many mansions: if it were not so, I would have told you. I go to prepare a place for you. And if I go and prepare a place for you, I will come again, and receive you unto myself; that where I am, there ye may be also." The promise of a prepared place with God in eternity provides hope and comfort as believers run their race of faith.

In conclusion, the checkered flag in NASCAR and the end of life for Christians share many parallels, both marking the culmination of a journey filled with challenges, growth, and perseverance. In NASCAR, the checkered flag signals the end of the race and the achievement of victory, reflecting the hard work, skill, and determination of the driver and their team. Similarly, the end of a Christian's life marks the beginning of eternity with Christ, the ultimate reward for a life of faith and perseverance. 2 Timothy 4:7-8 captures this sentiment beautifully: "I have fought a good fight, I have finished my course, I have kept the faith: Henceforth there is laid up for me a crown of righteousness, which the Lord, the righteous judge, shall give me at that day: and not to me only, but unto all them also that love his appearing." By understanding the parallels between these two races, believers can draw inspiration and strength from the lessons learned on the track and apply them to their spiritual journey, ultimately finishing their race of faith with confidence and hope, looking forward to the promise of eternal life with God.

Chapter 23 Speed

SPEED IS ESSENTIAL in NASCAR and the Christian life, though they apply it differently. In NASCAR, drivers need speed to win races. The faster a car can go, the better its chances of crossing the finish line first. Achieving and maintaining high speeds involves several factors: the driver's skill, the car's engineering, the team's strategy, and the conditions of the track. Drivers must have quick reflexes, precise control, and the ability to make split-second decisions. The car must be designed for aerodynamics, have a powerful engine, and be maintained meticulously. The pit crew must perform rapid tire changes, refueling, and repairs. The team's strategy, including when to pit and how to manage the car's performance, is crucial. Track conditions, like weather and surface quality, also affect speed. A successful NASCAR driver combines all these elements to achieve the highest possible speed without losing control or safety. Speed is thrilling and captivating, attracting fans who enjoy the excitement of high-speed racing. It embodies the competitive spirit of NASCAR, where every fraction of a second counts, and drivers push their limits to be the fastest.

Similarly, in the Christian life, believers are called to be quick in doing good, though the focus is not on physical speed but on the promptness and eagerness to act in ways that honor God and serve others. Christians are encouraged to be swift to hear, slow to speak, and slow to wrath, as stated in James 1:19: "Wherefore, my beloved brethren, let every man be swift to hear, slow to speak, slow to wrath." This verse emphasizes the importance of being quick to listen and understand, taking time to consider words carefully, and controlling anger. Being swift to hear means being attentive and open to others' perspectives, showing empathy and understanding. This helps build strong relationships and fosters a supportive community. Being slow to speak involves thinking before speaking, ensuring words are kind, thoughtful, and constructive. This prevents misunderstandings and hurt feelings, promoting peace and harmony. Being slow to wrath means managing emotions and avoiding quick reactions that lead to conflict. It involves patience, forgiveness, and a calm approach to handling disagreements.

In the Christian context, speed also refers to the promptness in doing good deeds and responding to God's call. Believers are encouraged to act quickly in helping others, sharing the gospel, and living out their faith. This proactive approach reflects a heart dedicated to serving God and others. Proverbs 3:27 urges, "Withhold not good from them to whom it is due, when it is in the power of thine hand to do it." Christians are called to seize opportunities to do good, making the most of their time and resources to make a positive impact. This includes acts of kindness, generosity, and service, which demonstrate God's love and compassion to the world. Being quick in doing good also involves responding to God's guidance without hesitation. When believers feel called to a particular action, they are encouraged to obey promptly, trusting in God's plan and timing. This readiness to act shows faith and reliance on God's wisdom.

Both in NASCAR and the Christian life, speed involves a balance of quickness and control. In racing, drivers must balance speed with precision to avoid accidents and maintain control of their vehicle. Going too fast without control can lead to crashes and mistakes. Similarly, in the Christian life, being quick to do good must be balanced with wisdom and discernment. Acting impulsively without considering the consequences can lead to poor decisions and harm. Christians are encouraged to seek God's guidance and use wisdom in their actions, ensuring that their quick responses align with God's will and purpose. This balance ensures that their actions are effective and beneficial, promoting God's kingdom and helping others.

In NASCAR, speed also involves preparation and teamwork. Drivers and their teams spend countless hours preparing for races, fine-tuning the car, practicing on the track, and developing strategies. This preparation enables them to achieve high speeds safely and effectively. Similarly, in the Christian life, preparation and teamwork are essential for being quick in doing good. Believers need to prepare through prayer, studying the Bible, and seeking spiritual growth. This preparation equips them with the knowledge, strength, and guidance needed to act swiftly and wisely. Teamwork in the Christian community involves supporting one another, sharing burdens, and working together to accomplish God's work. Just as a NASCAR team collaborates to achieve the best performance, Christians are called to work together in unity, encouraging and helping each other to be effective in their faith and service.

In both contexts, speed requires endurance and perseverance. In NASCAR, maintaining high speeds throughout a race demands physical endurance from the driver and mechanical endurance from the car. The race can be long and grueling, testing the limits of both. Similarly, in the Christian life, believers need endurance to continue doing good, even when faced with challenges, fatigue, or opposition. Galatians 6:9 encourages, "And let us not be weary in well doing: for in due season we shall reap, if we faint not." This verse reminds Christians to persevere in their efforts, trusting that their faithful actions will yield positive results in God's timing. Endurance in the Christian life involves staying committed to God's call, remaining steadfast in faith, and continuing to serve others, even when it is difficult.

The concept of speed in the Christian life also involves a sense of urgency in sharing the gospel and advancing God's kingdom. Believers are called to spread the message of salvation quickly and passionately, recognizing the importance of reaching others with the good news of Jesus Christ. Matthew 28:19-20, known as the Great Commission, instructs, "Go ye therefore, and teach all nations, baptizing them in the name of the Father, and of the Son, and of the Holy Ghost: Teaching them to observe all things whatsoever I have commanded you: and, lo, I am with you alway, even unto the end of the world." This mission requires Christians to act with urgency, making the most of every opportunity to share their faith and demonstrate God's love.

In NASCAR, achieving speed also involves innovation and continuous improvement. Teams constantly seek ways to enhance their car's performance, experimenting with new technologies, materials, and techniques. This drive for innovation keeps the sport competitive and exciting.

Similarly, in the Christian life, believers are called to grow and improve continually, seeking to deepen their relationship with God and become more effective in their service. This involves being open to new experiences, learning from others, and embracing change when it aligns with God's will.

Ephesians 4:15 encourages growth, stating, "But speaking the truth in love, may grow up into him in all things, which is the head, even Christ." By continually seeking growth and improvement, Christians can become more effective in their faith journey and more capable of making a positive impact in the world.

Both in NASCAR and the Christian life, speed is accompanied by a sense of excitement and fulfillment. The thrill of high-speed racing captivates fans and drives competitors to push their limits. Similarly, the Christian life, when lived with a commitment to being swift in doing good, brings a sense of joy and fulfillment. Acts of kindness, service, and sharing God's love bring happiness to both the giver and the receiver. Proverbs 11:25 reflects this truth: "The liberal soul shall be made fat: and he that watereth shall be watered also himself." By being quick to do good, Christians experience the joy of fulfilling God's call and making a difference in the lives of others.

In conclusion, speed is a crucial element in NASCAR and the Christian life, though they apply it differently. In NASCAR, drivers need speed to win races, relying on skill, preparation, teamwork, and endurance to achieve high speeds safely and effectively. Similarly, Christians are called to be quick in doing good, acting promptly and eagerly to honor God and serve others. James 1:19 emphasizes the importance of being swift to hear, slow to speak, and slow to wrath, guiding believers to act with wisdom and discernment. By balancing quickness with control, preparing through spiritual disciplines, working together in unity, and persevering with endurance, Christians can navigate their faith journey effectively and make a positive impact. The urgency in sharing the gospel, continuous growth and improvement, and the joy of serving others reflect the excitement and fulfillment that come with being quick to do good. In both contexts, speed is not just about the physical act of moving quickly but about the readiness and willingness to act decisively and effectively, whether on the race track or in the journey of faith.

Chapter 24 Focus on the Goal

IN NASCAR, DRIVERS must maintain an intense focus on the finish line to navigate the high-speed and high-stakes environment effectively, mirroring the Christian life's focus on the ultimate goal of eternal life with God. Drivers concentrate on the finish line from the moment the race begins, dedicating their full attention to the track, their strategy, and their car's performance. They need to stay alert and ready to respond to any sudden changes, such as other cars' movements, weather conditions, and track dynamics. Distractions can lead to mistakes, crashes, or losing positions, so maintaining focus is crucial. This single-minded concentration helps them make quick, precise decisions that can lead to victory. Similarly, in the Christian life, believers are called to focus on the goal of eternal life with God, keeping their faith and actions aligned with this ultimate purpose. Philippians 3:13-14 encapsulates this focus: "Brethren, I count not myself to have apprehended: but this one thing I do, forgetting those things which are behind, and reaching forth unto those things which are before, I press toward the mark for the prize of the high calling of God in Christ Jesus." This verse encourages Christians to let go of past mistakes and distractions, continually striving towards the goal of eternal life and the fulfillment of God's calling.

In both contexts, maintaining focus requires discipline and commitment. NASCAR drivers train rigorously, both physically and mentally, to prepare for the demands of the race. They practice on different tracks, analyze past performances, and work closely with their teams to develop strategies. This preparation ensures that they can remain focused and perform at their best when it matters most. Similarly, Christians must engage in spiritual disciplines such as prayer, Bible study, and worship to stay focused on their faith journey. These practices help believers grow in their relationship with God, understand His will, and gain the strength needed to stay committed to their goal. Just as a driver's preparation is crucial for their success on the track, a Christian's spiritual preparation is vital for their journey of faith.

Both NASCAR drivers and Christians must also deal with distractions and challenges that can divert their focus from the goal. On the track, drivers face numerous distractions, such as the noise of the crowd, the pressure of competition, and the constant need to monitor their car's performance. They must tune out these distractions and remain concentrated on the finish line. Similarly, Christians encounter distractions in their daily lives that can shift their focus away from their spiritual goals. These distractions can include materialism, social pressures, and personal struggles. By staying rooted in their faith and continually seeking God's guidance, believers can overcome these distractions and keep their eyes on the prize of eternal life.

Perseverance is another essential quality for maintaining focus on the goal. NASCAR races are grueling, requiring drivers to maintain their focus and determination over long periods. They must persevere through physical fatigue, mechanical issues, and the psychological pressure of the competition. This perseverance helps them stay focused on the finish line, pushing through difficulties to achieve their goal. Similarly, Christians are called to persevere in their faith, even when faced with trials and temptations. James 1:12 encourages believers to persevere: "Blessed is the man that endureth temptation: for when he is tried, he shall receive the crown of life, which the Lord hath promised to them that love him." By persevering through challenges and staying committed to their faith, Christians can remain focused on their ultimate goal of eternal life with God.

Support and encouragement from others are crucial in maintaining focus. NASCAR drivers rely on their teams for support, including the pit crew, engineers, and strategists who help them stay on track and perform at their best. This teamwork and collaboration are essential for overcoming challenges and staying focused on the goal. Similarly, Christians rely on the support and encouragement of their fellow believers. The Christian community provides a network of support through prayer, accountability, and mutual encouragement. Hebrews 10:24-25 emphasizes the importance of this support: "And let us consider one another to provoke unto love and to good works: Not forsaking the assembling of ourselves together, as the manner of some is; but exhorting one another: and so much the more, as ye see the day approaching." By supporting and encouraging one another, believers can help each other stay focused on their spiritual goals.

Adaptability is also essential for maintaining focus on the goal. In NASCAR, drivers must adapt to changing conditions on the track, such as weather changes, tire wear, and the actions of other drivers. This adaptability allows them to adjust their strategy and maintain their focus on the finish line. Similarly, Christians must be adaptable in their spiritual journey, ready to adjust their plans and approaches as they seek God's guidance. Proverbs 3:5-6 encourages believers to trust in God's direction: "Trust in the LORD with all thine heart; and lean not unto thine own understanding. In all thy ways acknowledge him, and he shall direct thy paths." By being flexible and open to God's leading, Christians can navigate their spiritual race more effectively.

Both NASCAR drivers and Christians must also set their sights on the ultimate goal, keeping their eyes on the prize. In NASCAR, the goal is to cross the finish line first, achieving victory and earning points toward the championship. This goal drives drivers to push their limits, stay focused, and persevere through challenges. Similarly, Christians run their race with the ultimate goal of eternal life with God. Philippians 3:13-14 captures this forward-looking determination: "Brethren, I count not myself to have apprehended: but this one thing I do, forgetting those things which are behind, and reaching forth unto those things which are before, I press toward the mark for the prize of the high calling of God in Christ Jesus." By keeping their eyes on the ultimate prize, Christians can stay motivated and committed to their faith journey.

In both NASCAR and the Christian life, maintaining focus on the goal involves learning and growth. NASCAR drivers continually learn from their experiences, gaining new insights and improving their skills. They analyze their performance, learn from their mistakes, and refine their strategies. This ongoing process of learning and growth helps them stay focused on their goal and achieve greater success. Similarly, Christians are called to grow in their faith, gaining wisdom and deepening their understanding of God's Word. Each challenge and trial provides an opportunity for growth and transformation, helping believers to mature in their faith and draw closer to God. Romans 5:3-4 speaks to this process of growth: "And not only so, but we glory in tribulations also: knowing that tribulation worketh patience; And patience, experience; and experience, hope." By embracing the lessons and growth opportunities along the way, Christians can maintain their focus on their ultimate goal with greater purpose and determination.

Both NASCAR drivers and Christians must also practice selfdiscipline to maintain focus on their goals. In NASCAR, drivers must be disciplined in their training, diet, and lifestyle to ensure they are in peak physical and mental condition for racing. This discipline helps them stay focused and perform at their best. Similarly, Christians must practice self-discipline in their spiritual lives, dedicating time to prayer, Bible study, and worship. This discipline helps them stay focused on their faith journey and grow in their relationship with God. 1 Corinthians 9:25-27 illustrates the importance of discipline: "And every man that striveth for the mastery is temperate in all things. Now they do it to obtain a corruptible crown; but we an incorruptible. I therefore so run, not as uncertainly; so fight I, not as one that beateth the air: But I keep under my body, and bring it into subjection: lest that by any means, when I have preached to others, I myself should be a castaway."

In conclusion, maintaining focus on the goal is crucial in both NASCAR and the Christian life. In NASCAR, drivers focus on the finish line, dedicating their full attention to the track, their strategy, and their car's performance.

They must stay alert, make quick decisions, and adapt to changing conditions, all while pushing their limits to achieve victory. Similarly, Christians are called to focus on the goal of eternal life with God, keeping their faith and actions aligned with this ultimate purpose. Philippians 3:13-14 encapsulates this focus: "Brethren, I count not myself to have apprehended: but this one thing I do, forgetting those things which are behind, and reaching forth unto those things which are before, I press toward the mark for the prize of the high calling of God in Christ Jesus." By practicing discipline, perseverance, adaptability, and resilience, and by relying on the support and encouragement of their fellow believers, Christians can maintain their focus on their ultimate goal and run their race of faith with confidence and determination.

78

Chapter 25 Sponsor

SPONSORS PLAY A CRUCIAL role in NASCAR, providing the financial backing and resources that drivers need to compete at the highest level. These sponsors fund the race teams, covering the costs of car development, travel, equipment, and more. In return, sponsors receive advertising and branding opportunities, with their logos prominently displayed on the race cars, driver uniforms, and various team gear. This relationship is mutually beneficial: the drivers and teams get the financial support they need to race competitively, and the sponsors gain visibility and exposure through the exciting world of NASCAR. Sponsors also often provide additional support through marketing and promotional efforts, helping to build the driver's and team's public profiles and fan bases. This support is essential for success in NASCAR, as it allows drivers to focus on their performance without worrying about financial constraints.

Similarly, in the Christian life, believers have God's support, which is far more significant and powerful than any earthly sponsor. God's support provides strength, guidance, and resources to help Christians navigate life's challenges and fulfill their spiritual calling. Philippians 4:13 encapsulates this support: "I can do all things through Christ which strengtheneth me." This verse reminds believers that with God's support, they can overcome any obstacle and achieve their spiritual goals. Just as NASCAR drivers rely on their sponsors for the resources and backing needed to compete, Christians rely on God for the strength and guidance to live out their faith and pursue their purpose.

In both NASCAR and the Christian life, preparation is essential. NASCAR drivers and their teams spend countless hours preparing for races, fine-tuning their cars, practicing on tracks, and developing strategies. This preparation is made possible through the support of their sponsors, who provide the necessary funding and resources. Similarly, Christians prepare for their spiritual journey through prayer, Bible study, worship, and fellowship with other believers. God's support enables this preparation, providing wisdom, insight, and the presence of the Holy Spirit to guide them. This preparation equips believers with the tools they need to face life's challenges and stay true to their faith.

Endurance is another critical aspect in both contexts. NASCAR races are long and grueling, requiring drivers to maintain their focus and performance over extended periods. The support from sponsors ensures that the drivers have the best equipment, training, and resources to endure these demanding races. Similarly, Christians are called to endure in their faith, persevering through trials and hardships. God's support provides the strength and resilience needed to endure, encouraging believers to stay committed to their spiritual journey. James 1:12 highlights the importance of endurance: "Blessed is the man that endureth temptation: for when he is tried, he shall receive the crown of life, which the

Lord hath promised to them that love him."

Focus is essential for success in both NASCAR and the Christian life. NASCAR drivers must keep their eyes on the finish line, staying concentrated on their strategy and performance. The support from sponsors allows them to focus on racing, without the distraction of financial worries. Similarly, Christians must keep their focus on their ultimate goal of eternal life with God. Philippians 3:13-14 emphasizes this focus: "Brethren, I count not myself to have apprehended: but this one thing I do, forgetting those things which are behind, and reaching forth unto those things which are before, I press toward the mark for the prize of the high calling of God in Christ Jesus." God's support helps believers maintain this focus, providing clarity and direction as they navigate their faith journey.

Teamwork is another vital component in both contexts. In NASCAR, success depends on the coordinated efforts of the entire team, including the driver, pit crew, engineers, and strategists. Sponsors support the team by funding these crucial roles and providing the resources needed for effective teamwork. Similarly, Christians rely on the support and encouragement of their fellow believers. The Christian community works together to support one another, share burdens, and grow in faith. Hebrews 10:24-25 highlights the importance of this support: "And let us consider one another to provoke unto love and to good works: Not forsaking the assembling of ourselves together, as the manner of some is; but exhorting one another: and so much the more, as ye see the day approaching." God's support underpins this teamwork, providing the foundation for unity and cooperation among believers.

In both NASCAR and the Christian life, the support from sponsors and God, respectively, enables individuals to achieve their goals and reach their full potential. NASCAR drivers, with the backing of their sponsors, can push their limits, innovate, and strive for victory. Similarly, Christians, with God's support, can grow in their faith, overcome challenges, and fulfill their spiritual calling. Philippians 4:13 serves as a powerful reminder of this divine support: "I can do all things through Christ which strengtheneth me."

Sponsors in NASCAR often provide more than just financial support; they offer encouragement and motivation. They celebrate successes with the team and provide a sense of security and confidence. This support boosts the morale of the driver and team, helping them stay motivated and focused. Similarly, God's support provides encouragement and motivation for Christians. Through His Word, the presence of the Holy Spirit, and the encouragement of fellow believers, God uplifts and strengthens His people, helping them stay motivated in their spiritual journey.

Both NASCAR drivers and Christians face challenges and setbacks, but with the support of their sponsors and God, they can overcome these obstacles. In NASCAR, a wellfunded team can recover from a crash or mechanical failure, make necessary repairs, and get back on track. Similarly, Christians can face life's difficulties with the assurance that God's support will help them overcome. Isaiah 41:10 offers comfort and reassurance: "Fear thou not; for I am with thee: be not dismayed; for I am thy God: I will strengthen thee; yea, I will help thee; yea, I will uphold thee with the right hand of my righteousness."

Innovation and continuous improvement are also crucial in both contexts. NASCAR teams constantly seek ways to improve their car's performance, innovate with new technologies, and refine their strategies. Sponsors support these efforts by funding research and development. Similarly, Christians are called to grow and improve continually, seeking to deepen their relationship with God and become more effective in their service. Ephesians 4:15 encourages this growth: "But speaking the truth in love, may grow up into him in all things, which is the head, even Christ." God's support enables this continuous improvement, providing the guidance and strength needed to grow in faith.

In both NASCAR and the Christian life, the ultimate goal is achieved through the combined efforts of the individual and the support they receive. For NASCAR drivers, reaching the finish line and achieving victory is a team effort, made possible by the support of their sponsors. Similarly, Christians reach their ultimate goal of eternal life with God through their faith, actions, and the support of God. Philippians 4:13 encapsulates this truth: "I can do all things through Christ which strengtheneth me."

In conclusion, sponsors play a crucial role in NASCAR, providing the financial backing and resources that drivers need to compete at the highest level. This support allows drivers to focus on their performance, endure the demands of racing, and achieve their goals. Similarly, Christians have God's support, which provides strength, guidance, and resources to navigate life's challenges and fulfill their spiritual calling. Philippians 4:13 reminds believers of this divine support: "I can do all things through Christ which strengtheneth me." Both in NASCAR and the Christian life, preparation, endurance, focus, teamwork, and support from sponsors and God, respectively, are essential for success. By understanding these parallels, believers can draw inspiration and strength from the lessons learned on the track and apply them to their spiritual journey, ultimately achieving their goals and fulfilling their purpose with the support of God.

Conclusion

As we draw to the conclusion of our journey through the parallels between the Christian life and NASCAR, it becomes clear that the principles that guide success on the racetrack also apply powerfully to our walk of faith. Both pursuits require careful preparation, unwavering endurance, sharp focus, committed teamwork, and robust support. By examining these shared aspects, we find practical and spiritual lessons that can inspire and strengthen us in our daily lives.

Preparation is a cornerstone for both NASCAR drivers and Christians. Just as drivers spend countless hours training, fine-tuning their cars, and strategizing for races, Christians are called to prepare their hearts and minds for their spiritual journey. This preparation involves immersing ourselves in God's Word, praying, and seeking His guidance. As the Bible encourages in 2 Timothy 2:15, "Study to shew thyself approved unto God, a workman that needeth not to be ashamed, rightly dividing the word of truth." Through diligent preparation, we equip ourselves to handle life's challenges with wisdom and grace.

Endurance is another vital quality. NASCAR races are long and grueling, testing drivers' physical and mental stamina. Similarly, the Christian journey is marked by trials and tribulations that test our faith and perseverance. James 1:12 reminds us, "Blessed is the man that endureth temptation: for when he is tried, he shall receive the crown of life, which the Lord hath promised to them that love him." By enduring through difficulties, we develop resilience and deepen our faith, ultimately drawing closer to the promise of eternal life.

Focus is essential in both contexts. NASCAR drivers must maintain their concentration on the finish line, blocking out distractions and staying true to their strategy. In the same way, Christians are called to keep their eyes on Jesus, the author and finisher of our faith. Hebrews 12:1-2 urges us, "Let us run with patience the race that is set before us, Looking unto Jesus the author and finisher of our faith; who for the joy that was set before him endured the cross, despising the shame, and is set down at the right hand of the throne of God." By focusing on Christ and His promises, we can navigate life's distractions and remain steadfast in our spiritual journey.

Teamwork plays a crucial role in both NASCAR and the Christian life. Drivers depend on their pit crews and support teams for success, mirroring how Christians rely on the fellowship and encouragement of other believers. Ephesians 4:16 illustrates this beautifully: "From whom the whole body fitly joined together and compacted by that which every joint supplieth, according to the effectual working in the measure of every part, maketh increase of the body unto the edifying of itself in love." Through unity and mutual support, we strengthen each other and build a vibrant, loving community that can achieve great things for God's kingdom.

Finally, support is fundamental. NASCAR drivers depend on their sponsors for the resources and backing needed to compete at the highest level. Likewise, Christians rely on God's unwavering support to sustain them through their journey. Philippians 4:13 reassures us, "I can do all things through Christ which strengtheneth me." With God's support, we can overcome any obstacle, achieve our spiritual goals, and live out our faith boldly and confidently.

In conclusion, the journey of a NASCAR driver and the path of a Christian share striking similarities, with both requiring preparation, endurance, focus, teamwork, and support. By applying these principles to our spiritual lives, we can run our race with greater purpose and determination. Let us press toward the mark for the prize of the high calling of God in Christ Jesus (Philippians 3:14), confident in His guidance and support. As we navigate the twists and turns of life's racetrack, may we remain steadfast, encouraged by the knowledge that we are not alone, but part of a larger community of believers, supported by God's boundless love and grace. With our eyes fixed on the ultimate finish line, we can look forward to the joy and fulfillment that comes from running our race well and hearing those cherished words, "Well done, thou good and faithful servant" (Matthew 25:21).

Don't miss out!

Visit the website below and you can sign up to receive emails whenever Joshua Rhoades publishes a new book. There's no charge and no obligation.

https://books2read.com/r/B-A-AJLBB-NZEQD

BOOKS2READ

Connecting independent readers to independent writers.

Did you love *Driven By Faith: Motor Racing Inspired Christian Life*? Then you should read *HOOK, LINE & SAVIOUR - Faith Reflections from Fishing*[1] by Joshua Rhoades!

"Hook, Line, and Saviour: Faith Reflections from Fishing" is an engaging book for both the young and not so young, blending fishing with Christian faith principles. Through 24 chapters, it draws parallels between fishing techniques and the Christian life, making spiritual lessons relatable and fun.It starts with "Chapter 1 - Research and Knowledge," emphasizing the importance of understanding and preparation in both fishing and faith. "Chapter 2 - Choosing the Right Gear" draws a parallel between selecting the right fishing tools and using spiritual tools like prayer and scripture."Chapter 3 - Learning to Cast" highlights the need for skill and practice, comparing it to sharing one's faith. "Chapter 4 - Understanding Weather Conditions" connects the importance of weather awareness for fishing to understanding spiritual and emotional climates. "Chapter 5 - Tide and Water Currents" uses tides to illustrate how life's changes can be navigated with trust in God.In "Chapter 6 - Selecting the Right Bait," using the right bait attracts fish, just as kindness and love draw others to faith. "Chapter 7 - Tackle Box Organization" underscores being spiritually organized and prepared. "Chapter 8 - Knot Tying" emphasizes building strong relationships with God and others, like tying secure knots."Chapter 9 - Boat Maintenance" compares maintaining faith through prayer to keeping a boat in good condition. "Chapter 10 - Fishing Regulations" highlights adhering to God's commandments, like following fishing laws. "Chapter 11 - Fish Finder Technology" parallels using technology to locate fish with seeking guidance through prayer."Chapter 12 - Patience and Persistence" teaches that both fishing and faith require waiting and perseverance. "Chapter 13 - Observation Skills" encourages attentiveness to God's work, like a fisherman watches for fish. "Chapter 14 - Casting Techniques" and "Chapter 15 - Reeling Techniques" relate fishing skills to guiding others to faith."Chapter 16 - Fishing Ethics" emphasizes integrity and honesty in fishing and life. "Chapter 17 - Adapting to Seasons" discusses embracing God's plan through life's phases. "Chapter 18 - Using Scents and Attractants" highlights living a life that draws others to Christ."Chapter 19 - Fishing Logs" suggests keeping a faith journal to track growth. "Chapter 20 - Joining a Fishing Community" underscores fellowship and support. "Chapter 21 - Safety Precautions" parallels physical safety measures in fishing with spiritual protection."Chapter 22 - Learning from Experts" encourages seeking wisdom from mentors. "Chapter 23 - Adapting to Different Waters" relates to being adaptable in life. "Chapter 24 - Staying

1. https://books2read.com/u/brjDGE

2. https://books2read.com/u/brjDGE

Informed" emphasizes continuous spiritual growth.Overall, "Hook, Line, and Saviour" makes learning about faith accessible and enjoyable. Through practical application it encourages spiritual growth and helps readers apply Christian principles in daily life. This book is an adventurous guide that deepens faith through the exciting world of fishing, making spiritual growth enriching and fun.